Under the General Editorship of

Jesse W. Markham

Harvard University

Houghton Mifflin Adviser in Economics

Decision Making for Economic Development

Text and Cases

Gustav F. Papanek
Harvard University

Daniel M. Schydlowsky
Harvard University

Joseph J. Stern
Harvard University

Houghton Mifflin Company · **Boston**

New York · Atlanta · Geneva, Illinois · Dallas · Palo Alto

Printed in the U.S.A.

Library of Congress Catalog Card Number: 74–128709

ISBN: 0–395–05036–7

Editor's Introduction

The systematic study of economic development has been in its ascendency since the end of World War II. Courses in the subject have proliferated in college curricula at the undergraduate and graduate levels. Programs and institutes concentrating on economic development have sprung up on many university campuses, paralleling and responding to mounting student enrollment and faculty specialization. The increased preoccupation with economic development has significantly shaped the design of national policies and international institutions.

The proximate cause for this allocation of greater intellectual and political energy and economic resources to the problems of development can be easily identified: as a consequence of the crumbling of empires after World War II, the number of nations greatly increased. The vast majority of the new nations were created out of the relatively undeveloped regions of Africa and Asia. The contrast between what were popularly designated as the "have" and the "have not" nations was thus brought into bold relief; the contrast evoked the aspirations of the "have nots" and the feeling of obligation, duty, responsibility, humanitarianism, and possibly shame, of the "haves."

Economists, true to the nature of their discipline, propounded theories of development. As a consequence, the theoretical literature, for at least a decade or so, stayed a considerable distance ahead of that concerned with the practical analysis of actual development problems. While the field was in its infancy, Professor Edward Mason founded the Harvard Pakistan Project—which in 1962 became the Harvard Development Advisory Service—to further our understanding of economic development at both the theoretical and operational levels. Harvard became one of the major centers for research and training in development economics.

Dr. Papanek, a long-time member of the Harvard Pakistan Project, and since 1964 the Director of the Development Advisory Service, has developed, with his associates, Daniel Schydlowsky and Joseph Stern, the text and case material contained in this volume in the course of their many years of involvement in problems of economic development. Since 1966 they have successfully applied the case method to the teaching of economic development in the Department of Economics and the Kennedy School of Government at Harvard. The classroom-tested volume that has evolved from their first-hand experience with problems of development, and from their teaching, is a welcome addition to the literature in one of the most important areas of economics. It should be of immense value to those who teach and study the subject.

Jesse W. Markham

Harvard University

Preface

This book has evolved from a successful experiment in applying the case method to the teaching of economic development begun by Gustav F. Papanek and Daniel M. Schydlowsky under the auspices of the Department of Economics and the Kennedy School of Government at Harvard in the Spring Term of 1966. Over the years, the case material has been improved, clarified, and replaced under the beneficial influence of student reaction, the addition of Joseph J. Stern to the teaching team and the availability of new experience.

The case material is taken from the experience of the Development Advisory Service of the Center of International Affairs of Harvard, which has worked with the planning agencies of the governments of Pakistan and Colombia, among others, and from Daniel M. Schydlowsky's experience as adviser to the Central Reserve Bank of Peru. To both institutions, to our students over the years and to Richard D. Mallon, who made valuable comments at many stages of the drafting, go our sincere thanks. We are also grateful to Sophia Magoulias and Margaret Wehner for assistance in managing the administration of the case-study material.

Contents

Tables Accompanying Country Backgrounds

Decision Making: The Case Study Approach

1

Few areas of economic analysis have grown as rapidly as the field of economic development in terms of interest, the development of analytical tools, and the number of practitioners. The demand for economists specifically trained to assist development efforts has resulted in a proliferation of training programs and courses dealing with the theoretical and practical aspects of planning methodology. Often, however, there is a wide gulf between those who approach the problems of development from a theoretical point of view and those who deal with the issues actually facing the less developed nations. The theorists tend to present their analysis in terms of elegant models characterized by strong assumptions about certainty and about the availability of comprehensive data and they tend to neglect the difficult task of defining the goals of a society, postulating instead very simple objectives. Those who proceed from a basis of practical experience, on the other hand, tend to view the development process as a series of special cases often neglecting to notice the similarities which many relationships bear to each other from the point of view of economic analysis. As a result, those who must eventually deal with problems of development and planning in their actual setting often do not know how to apply their knowledge of theory to the case at hand.

The purpose of the case study approach is to bridge this gulf. Each case poses a specific problem or set of issues whose resolution requires the application of precise analytical techniques. However, the analysis must be tailored to the availability of statistical data and the proposed solution must take account of uncertainty and the constraints which the social and political framework and objectives place on policy recommendations. Each case generates a search for the theoretical and methodological approaches applicable to the problem, but provides a concrete scenario that forces the adaptation of general principles to a concrete case, with all the limitations this imposes on a decision maker.

Governmental Decision Making

The decision makers in these cases are government officials in the central economic staff (often called a planning agency) of less developed countries. They are therefore concerned with the effect of their decisions on the economy as a whole. The question they are expected to answer is: given the objectives of the society, some of which are probably conflicting and which are usually stated by the political leadership in a fuzzy way, what decisions are most likely to permit the greatest progress towards these objectives? Such decision makers are expected to come up with firm recommendations. They would soon lose their jobs if they do not, pleading inadequate data, lack of time or imprecise instructions.

Their recommendations are expected to take account of the political, social and institutional constraints known to them (and specified in the cases that follow), but within these constraints, the recommendations are to be based on economic criteria and judgments. For example, if the issue is whether a steel mill or pulp mill should be constructed, the economists (and the solvers of cases in this book) should take into account that money wages cannot be reduced for political and institutional reasons. However, given this constraint, they should calculate the economic costs and benefits and base their recommendations on this calculation. Whether the steel mill should be preferred for prestige or political reasons, even if it is less desirable in economic terms, is a subsequent decision, better left to the political leadership. After all, the politician does not employ the economist to second-guess him on political matters, but to provide economic expertise.

The Choice of Cases

Obviously, the number of interesting decisions made by policy makers in less developed countries is too large to be handled in one academic year. It was therefore necessary to choose a limited number of situations for embodiment in cases. The criteria used for this selection were:

1. The cases should cover a wide spectrum of topics.

2. They should touch on decisions common to many less developed countries.

3. They should be based on real occurrences.

4. They should be amenable to solution through economic analysis. They may have more than one appropriate solution but must have at least one.

Bearing these guidelines in mind, the cases deal with four broad areas of economic analysis: investment decisions; policies for the external sector; fiscal and monetary policy; and, problems of macroeconomic planning.

To provide a realistic framework for decision making, cases are drawn from three countries: Colombia, Pakistan and Peru. This does not imply that these countries are unique or deserving of special attention. Rather, by limiting the amount of required background information it is possible to focus on the general analysis which is of primary concern. A brief introduction and a set of appropriate statistical data are provided for each of the countries. The country descriptions are sufficient to provide a realistic framework against which the policy decision maker can operate. The statistical data reflect the weaknesses and lack of completeness often found in the raw material with which an analyst must work. Although references are given to other sources of statistical material, all the data available are almost never sufficient to reach conclusions with "full information." In this respect the cases simply reflect the actual situation of decision makers: they always face a lack of adequate information.

A number of cases deal with situations and decisions that actually occurred some time ago. However, the actual time period of the case is really not relevant. The basic analytic questions posed and tools used to decide them remain valid. The use of hindsight could provide an important advantage in dealing with decisions taken some time ago, especially for cases which depend crucially on projecting future economic situations. For instance, the decision on whether to allow a foreign private investor to develop Peru's copper resources is based on the situation in 1953. A knowledge of actual performance of the world copper market, available today, would greatly have eased the decision in 1953. But this information clearly was not available at that time and hence cannot be used in deciding the case. In short, each case must be resolved given the information which was available at the time the issue was posed.

In many of the cases it was necessary to abstract from some of the complications present in the real situation from which they are drawn in order to reduce the problem to one of manageable classroom size. Otherwise the pedagogical usefulness of the cases would have been severely impaired and the computational burden on the students increased for no valid purpose. A consequence of these simplifications is that the conclusions from the cases are not readily transferable to their real counterparts. Thus, for example, the classroom decision on Case 3 is not applicable readily to the real Tarbela complex with its 20 volumes of project documents.

The Cases

Although the case study method is frequently used in law and business school courses, it is unfamiliar to those studying economics. Therefore, before proceeding to the first set of major cases, two brief quantitative exercises are provided. The first deals with the problem of determining the historical growth rate of agriculture in order to project future targets, the second deals with the selection of a proper price index to deflate current export earnings. Although these introductory cases do not deal with any profound economic issue, they do highlight the potentials of the case study method. Each poses a specific set of questions and provides a limited amount of information. Alternative initial policy positions are posited and the task is to bring economic analysis to bear on the justification, partial or complete, of these alternative positions. As in all the cases which follow, none of the original positions can be rejected out of hand, although in the initial exercises the proposed solutions are presented in a more extreme manner than will be true later. Finally, as in a number of cases, the first of the introductory exercises has no clear solution. At best a certain position will have more merit, from an economic and a policy standpoint, than alternative solutions. But, as in reality, those who reach alternative conclusions defend their positions with arguments of considerable intellectual merit.

After the introductory exercises the first set of cases deal with the social choice among investments. The point of view is that of a Planning Commission or Development Ministry that has control over private as well as public investment. This control is exercised either through investment licensing or through the provision of incentives (tax holidays, import license or duty exemptions, and so forth) without which private investment is significantly less attractive. Three specific decisions are analysed: (a) the choice between two industrial projects; (b) the choice between a large multipurpose water control project and an industrial complex represented by the preferred choice in (a); and (c) the giving of a mining concession to foreign investors. The first case serves to introduce social benefit-cost accounting. It takes up the choice of objectives, the social valuation of output and factors of production and the handling of risk and uncertainty. For simplicity, the consideration of trade-offs over time are deferred to the second case where the choice of a discount rate is crucial to the outcome. In addition, the second case also requires dealing with externalities, savings and reinvestment and the valuation of goods and services not traded internationally (for example, electricity). The last case of this section uses the analysis developed previously and applies it to the evaluation of a concession agreement with a foreign mining company.

The second set of cases focuses on the central issue of a country's international economic policy. Case 5 requires the design of an export promotion policy and requires an understanding of the concept of comparative advantage and its measurement, both in the short and in the long run. Furthermore, input-output methodology and foreign trade multiplier theory are introduced and used to evaluate the different policy alternatives. Case 6 examines the other side of the trade account by concentrating on import controls. Using the principles established previously, this case calls for designing a policy to restrict imports in a fashion best suited to achieve a number of primary and secondary goals. The advantages and disadvantages of direct controls (such as import licenses) as against indirect ones (such as tariffs) are introduced. The final case in this section calls for integrating export and import policy as well as developing an appropriate policy for the remaining items of the overall balance of payments.

The third group of cases focuses on short run macroeconomic policy questions and brings fiscal and monetary issues into play. The first case deals with monetary policy and posits the classical question of the appropriate size of the expansion of the money supply. The solution requires the prepa-

ration of a monetary balance sheet for the economy together with supporting balance of payments and fiscal forecasts. The following case concen-
trates on the problem of an acute fiscal crisis: a fiscal deficit must be reduced
and the tax options are limited. The question is "which expenditures, if
any, should be reduced and what taxes, if any, should be raised?" The
answer which emerges is used together with the solution to the monetary
case in dealing with the final case of this section. Here the problem is to
plan a devaluation, determining a new exchange rate as well as a set of
complementary stabilization measures consisting of a monetary and fiscal
package. Throughout these cases the problem of structural inflation is
eschewed, in part because it has not in fact been very important in the
Peruvian context, and in part because the interdependencies created by its
presence makes the policy problems well nigh impossible to solve in a classroom situation, if not in reality.

The final section presents three problems of long term macroeconomic
planning. The first of these raises the question of the proper relationship
between internal and external relative prices in the context of a successful
agricultural program. The internal terms of trade between agriculture and
the urban sector, and their relationship to international prices, is certainly
one of the most important strategy questions for many countries. Political
considerations often play a paramount role, but the economic consequences
of a decision in this area can be neglected only at great cost. The second
case in the section ventures into fairly uncharted territory and presents the
problem of choosing a formal planning model. The construction of models
has made vast strides in the last decade, but application has so far lagged.
An important question with respect to application is the nature of the
formal model to use; how ambitious, how sophisticated it is possible and
desirable to be. Finally, the last case raises a number of issues in the choice
of a strategy of economic development. Much of the early literature on
development was preoccupied by questions on the best strategy—balanced
or unbalanced, emphasis on agriculture or industry or education and health
—but it gave little guidance to governments on how to decide such issues.
Yet governments do decide them and the case is concerned with the contribution of economic analysis to such decisions. The other major aspect
of the case, the extent and kind of government intervention in the economy,
is a hotly debated ideological issue crucial to the functioning of the economy.
Although noneconomic factors loom large in decisions, economic implications cannot be ignored and it is with these that the case is concerned.

The essence of the case study method is to examine alternative logical
positions, given limited information and uncertainties; to reach a policy
recommendation based on economic analysis, but fully cognizant of the
limitations imposed by social and political constraints; and to defend conclusions and recommendations, not because they are the only logically correct position, but because, given the entire spectrum of alternatives, they
appear to be the best possible from the perspective of the government policy
maker.

Case 1A: Measurement of Growth: Crop Production in East Pakistan

During the 1950s, crop production in East Pakistan was growing, at best, only about as fast as population. This situation has improved in the 1960s. By 1965 some observers go so far as to talk of an "agricultural revolution." The more cautious analysts regard such a characterization of the situation as a substantial overstatement of reality. The Planning Commission is engaged in making projections on the likely growth rate for the economy as part of the planning exercise being undertaken in conjunction with the preparation of the Third Five Year Plan (1965–1970). Some agreement on what has happened is of importance in making projections for East Pakistan whose agriculture constitutes over 50 per cent of gross regional product and over 20 per cent of Pakistan's gross national product.

The value of major crop production in East Pakistan for the period 1947/48 to 1964/65 is shown in Table 1A–1. In order to reach some quantitative agreement on a possible future growth rate, logarithmic trends were fitted to the data. The results are shown in Table 1A–2.

In addition, an analysis of the causal factors in the growth of agriculture in the 1960s suggests that a number of quantifiable factors would explain an increase in the growth of crop production of about 2.2 per cent per annum (see Table 1A–3). If additional labor inputs, improved technology, and the interaction among inputs had been considered also, the "explained" growth rate would have been higher.

The optimists suggest that in forecasting the growth of crop output the growth rate for 1957/58 to 1964/65 should be used. They justify their choice on statistical grounds, arguing that a trend calculated for a period of ten years is more reliable, since it is based on a greater number of observations, than one calculated for only an eight year period.

The pessimists argue that the trend calculated for 1959/60 to 1964/65 is a more appropriate base. They point out that a new government came into power in late 1958 and that the effects of new policies were not felt before late 1959. Furthermore, they point out that the analysis of causal factors in the growth rate seems to suggest that a lower rate is likely to be more appropriate.

Finally, a third group of analysts argue that regardless of which time period is chosen, the raw data should first be "adjusted" to take account of the severe year-to-year fluctuations in output which still plague East Pakistan's agricultural sector. These fluctuations, they note, are primarily due to weather conditions, monsoons and cyclones, thus reflecting factors that are beyond the control of the farmers. Hence, any effort to derive the "real" rate of growth in agriculture should be based on data which has been adjusted to eliminate these noneconomic factors. Use of a three-year moving average procedure is suggested as a means of smoothing the raw data.

Table 1A–1 Value of Major Crops Produced in East Pakistan (Crores of Rupees—1959–60 prices)

Commodity	1947/48	1948/49	1949/50	1950/51	1951/52	1952/53	1953/54	1954/55	1955/56
Rice	397.4	452.6	435.2	433.2	415.5	432.7	486.4	447.7	376.6
Grain	2.4	2.4	2.4	2.2	2.4	2.5	2.5	3.0	2.1
Sugar cane	14.7	15.3	13.9	15.0	15.4	16.5	17.9	16.6	17.8
Rape and mustard seed	7.0	7.4	7.7	8.0	8.9	9.2	8.0	9.4	9.3
Jute	88.9	71.2	43.3	78.0	82.3	88.7	46.9	60.6	72.7
Tea	8.4	10.3	11.7	11.4	14.1	15.4	15.6	15.0	15.8
Tobacco	9.6	9.8	9.5	9.3	9.7	10.6	10.6	11.4	8.6
Total	528.4	569.0	523.7	557.1	548.3	575.6	587.9	563.7	502.9

Commodity	1956/57	1957/58	1958/59	1959/60	1960/61	1961/62	1962/63	1963/64	1964/65 (preliminary)
Rice	482.8	448.2	408.3	500.3	561.5	534.8	515.0	616.8	610.0
Grain	1.6	1.6	1.8	1.4	1.7	1.7	1.6	1.6	1.8
Sugar cane	17.6	16.9	17.2	16.2	17.8	19.9	21.3	24.1	28.0
Rape and mustard seed	8.3	6.0	9.4	7.4	8.7	9.2	9.3	8.0	8.1
Jute	71.6	80.6	78.0	71.6	65.3	90.6	81.9	78.0	70.7
Tea	16.4	13.3	16.1	17.1	12.6	17.6	15.6	16.5	18.5
Tobacco	8.6	7.14	9.0	5.9	5.4	6.7	6.2	6.0	5.8
Total	606.9	574.0	539.8	619.9	673.0	680.5	650.9	751.0	742.9

Source: 1947/48–1963/64: Ministry of Agriculture; 1964/65: Pakistan Economic Survey.
Note: One crore = 10 million and one crore rupees = approximately $2 million.

Table 1A–2 *Regression Analysis Results[a]*

Time Period	Trend Equation ($\log Q = a + bt$)	R^2	$\bar{R}^2$ (adj)	T-ratio[b] (of slope)	F-ratio[b]	$D - W^c$
A. *Raw Data*						
(1) 1947/48–1964/65	$Q = 6.22 + 0.018t$ (0.0) (0.003)	0.65	0.61	5.46 (S)	29.9 (S)	1.45
(2) 1947/48–1957/58	$Q = 6.29 + 0.006t$ (0.03) (0.005)	0.12	0.07	1.13 (NS)	1.29 (NS)	2.73
(3) 1957/58–1964/65	$Q = 6.28 + 0.043t$ (0.04) (0.006)	0.83	0.77	5.32 (S)	28.28 (S)	2.61
(4) 1959/60–1964/65	$Q = 6.41 + 0.034t$ (0.04) (0.007)	0.72	0.58	3.23 (S)	10.41 (S)	2.95
B. *Three-year Moving Average*						
(5) 1948/49–1964/65	$Q = 6.24 + 0.017t$ (0.02) (0.002)	0.78	0.74	6.95 (S)	48.28 (S)	0.36*
(6) 1948/49–1957/58	$Q = 6.30 + 0.005t$ (0.01) (0.002)	0.42	0.27	2.38 (S)	5.69 (NS)	1.54
(7) 1957/58–1964/65	$Q = 6.28 + 0.038t$ (0.02) (0.004)	0.97	0.96	13.56 (S)	183.92 (S)	1.74
(8) 1959/60–1964/65	$Q = 6.33 + 0.042t$ (0.02) (0.004)	0.95	0.94	9.63 (S)	92.79 (S)	1.58

[a] All results rounded.
[b] All significance test done at 5% level; F one-tailed; T two-tailed.
[c] Durbin–Watson statistic.
S = significant
NS = not significant
* = serial correlation
Figures in parentheses are standard errors. Significance tests performed using nonrounded data.

The Planning Commission requests advice on which of the many possible growth rates is the most appropriate one to use in appraising the past performance of East Pakistan's agriculture sector and in forecasting the likely future level of agricultural production. Note that the problem is *not* to make a forecast, but only to estimate the rate of past growth which will be used as a benchmark in making a forecast. As stated earlier, developments after 1964/65 are *not* relevant to a solution.

Table 1A–3   *Causal Factors in Increased Crop Production—1959/60–1964/65*

Input	*(Annual Increase)* *Contribution to growth*
Fertilizer	0.5%
Irrigation, drainage	0.1
Plant protection	0.3
Improved seeds	0.5
Increase in cultivated area	1.3
Total	2.7%

Source: Walter P. Falcon and Carl H. Gotsch, "Lessons in Agricultural Development". Reprinted by permission of the publisher by Gustav F. Papanek, ed. *Development Policy: Theory and Practice*, Cambridge, Mass.: Harvard University Press, Copyright 1968 by the President and Fellows of Harvard College., p. 300.

Case 1B: The Construction of Index Numbers: Export Prices

Banania's balance of payments began to deteriorate in mid-1964. By early 1965 the loss of reserves was serious enough to require investigation. The President asked the Ministry of Trade to report on developments since 1950.

Two months later, the Ministry issued a report which stated, among other things, that: "It can be seen from the export price indices that over the last five years we have suffered a loss in export revenue equal to between four per cent and five per cent of our total earnings due to a decrease in the obtainable prices."

The two indices referred to are presented in Table 1B–1 and the underlying data from which they are constructed is given in Table 1B–3.

In the Cabinet discussions that followed the Ministry's of Trade report, the Head of the Central Office of Statistics claimed that the export prices had not deteriorated at all over the last years but had in fact risen. He presented the index shown in Table 1B–2 to substantiate his claim. This index is also constructed from the basic data in Table 1B–3.

At this point the President ordered all departments to submit information on how they compute their indices. The result is shown in Table 1B–4.

The President now calls you in and asks you:

1. Did export prices go up or down?

2. What is wrong with the index indicating the contrary direction of change?

3. On the basis of your answer to (2) which of the indices in Table 1B–4 would you definitely *not* recommend?

Table 1B–1 *Ministry of Trade Indices (Base: 1950)*

Formulas and Definitions

$$I_n^A = \frac{\sum_i P_{in} Q_{in}}{\sum_i P_{io} Q_{in}} \cdot 100 \qquad\qquad I_n^B = \frac{\sum_i P_{in} Q_{in}}{\sum_i P_{io} Q_{in}} \cdot 100$$

Q_i = proportion of value of commodity i in total	Q_i = tonnage of commodity i
P_i = price of commodity i	P_i = price of commodity i
n = current year	n = current year
o = base year	o = base year
I_n = index for year n	I_n = index for year n

Year	Index A	Index B
1950	100.0	100.0
1955	114.1	114.9
1960	119.2	121.2
1965	115.3	115.2

Table 1B–2   *Central Office of Statistics Index (Base: 1950)*

Formula and Definitions

$$I_n = \frac{\sum_i P_{in}Q_{io}}{\sum_i P_{io}Q_{io}} \cdot 100$$

Q_i = tonnage of commodity i
P_i = price of commodity i
n = current year
o = base year
I_n = Index for year n

Year	Index
1950	100.0
1955	115.7
1960	123.3
1965	126.0

Table 1B–3   *Prices and Quantities of Banania's Exports*

	Prices (U.S. Dollars per ton)		
Year	*Copper*	*Bananas*	*Jute*
1950	10.00	15.00	2.00
1955	10.00	19.00	3.00
1960	10.00	20.00	4.00
1965	10.00	21.00	4.00

	Quantities (tons)		
	Copper	*Bananas*	*Jute*
1950	50.00	26.66	50.00
1955	55.00	17.37	73.33
1960	62.50	18.75	62.50
1965	123.50	18.10	71.25

	Value of Exports (U.S. Dollars)			
	Copper	*Bananas*	*Jute*	*Total*
1950	500.00	400.00	100.00	1000.00
1955	550.00	330.00	220.00	1100.00
1960	625.00	375.00	250.00	1250.00
1965	1235.00	380.00	285.00	1900.00

Table 1B–4   *Formulas in Use in Various Departments*

A)   *Value weighted:*

$$I_n^1 = \frac{\sum P_n Q_n}{\sum P_o Q_n} \cdot 100 \qquad\qquad I_n^5 = \left[\sum \left\{\frac{P_n}{P_{n-1}}\right\} Q_n\right] I_{n-1}^5 \cdot 100$$

$$I_n^2 = \frac{\sum P_n Q_o}{\sum P_o Q_o} \cdot 100 \qquad\qquad I_n^6 = \left[\sum \left\{\frac{P_n}{P_{n-1}}\right\} Q_{n-1}\right] I_{n-1}^6 \cdot 100$$

$$I_n^3 = \sum \left\{\frac{P_n}{P_o}\right\} Q_n \cdot 100 \qquad\qquad I_n^7 = \left[\sum \left\{\frac{P_n}{P_{n-1}}\right\} Q_o\right] I_{n-1}^7 \cdot 100$$

$$I_n^4 = \sum \left\{\frac{P_n}{P_o}\right\} Q_o \cdot 100$$

B)   *Quantity weighted:*

$$I_n^8 = \frac{\sum P_n Q_n}{\sum P_o Q_n} \cdot 100$$

$$I_n^9 = \frac{\sum P_n Q_o}{\sum P_o Q_o} \cdot 100$$

$$I_n^{10} = \sum \frac{P_n}{P_o} \cdot \frac{Q_n}{\sum Q_n} = \frac{1}{\sum Q_n} \sum \left\{\frac{P_n}{P_o}\right\} Q_n \cdot 100$$

$$I_n^{11} = \sum \frac{P_n}{P_o} \cdot \frac{Q_o}{\sum Q_o} = \frac{1}{\sum Q_o} \sum \left\{\frac{P_n}{P_o}\right\} Q_o \cdot 100$$

Note: All summations are over the commodities i; therefore the commodity subscript has been suppressed.

Suggested Readings

1. Allen, R. G. D. "Index Numbers of Volume and Price." *International Trade Statistics.* Edited by R. G. D. Allen and J. Edward Ely. New York: John Wiley & Sons, 1963, chapter 10.

2. Lipsey, Robert E. *Price and Quantity Trends in the Foreign Trade of the United States.* National Bureau of Economic Research. Princeton: Princeton University Press, 1963, chapters 4 and 5.

Investment Decisions
and Project Selection

Introduction

Private investors clearly have criteria for deciding on the industries into which they will put their funds. These criteria would usually include the expected profitability of different investments, though they usually are not limited to this criterion. We are concerned, however, with the criteria to be applied by a government planning agency. The question is which of the alternative investments will achieve the greatest progress towards the economic objectives of the society as spelled out by the Planning Commission.

If the society has a multiplicity of objectives, the problem of weighing each objective eventually arises. If no weights are assigned, it becomes impossible to provide quantitative criteria for the choice of investments since one project is likely to achieve the greatest progress toward one of the objectives, while another is better in achieving another objective. Since many countries' objectives include at least the contribution of an investment to national income (or consumption), to foreign exchange availability and to employment, weighting can be difficult.

Clearly one objective of most countries is to increase the goods and services available to their citizens. But in comparing the output of several investments the question immediately arises of the prices that are to be used. In calculating gross benefits should each ton or each unit be valued at the price for which it is now sold in the market of the country; or the market price minus the taxes paid by consumers and producers; or the price for which the good can be imported (c.i.f.) or for which it could be exported (f.o.b.); or should some expected future price be used; and, in the case of subsidized exports is the appropriate price one with or without the subsidy? If the investment will increase the availability of a good so that its price declines, is the appropriate price the one before or after the decline? And if the price which is used is drawn from the international market, at what rate is its dollar price to be translated into local currency?

Once the price has been selected there is a good deal of uncertainty about possible changes in the price. Natural catastrophes or exceptionally favorable natural circumstances—as well as technological change, change in tastes or new discoveries—can produce sharp increases or declines in prices. Some investments are simply more risky than others. How are these risks and uncertainties to be taken into account?

Similar questions arise in calculating the costs of an investment project. The value to the society of some of the factors and inputs used in the project may not be given by their price in the market. The private investor is concerned with the wage he has to pay his workers, but the government planner in an economy where much of the labor force is unemployed may believe that the wage actually paid greatly overstates the cost to the society of employing some of the unemployed. On the other hand, a dollar's worth of foreign exchange spent may be considered worth more to the economy than the value indicated by the official exchange rate. And how should one value raw materials available in the country that would remain unused in the absence of the investment—say wild bamboo. Finally should any such "shadow" or "accounting" prices, as distinguished from those that prevail in the market, reflect the situation at the time the investment is started, or finished, or when it wears out of somewhere in between?

Furthermore, part of any given project may be financed out of resources available only for use in this project, for example, private foreign investment or suppliers' credit. Should such resources be considered part of the country's investment or a component of current costs? If the latter, what implications arise for a purely private foreign investment project? In such cases domestic investment costs would be nil and the denominator of the benefit/cost ratio vanishes.

Once the economic costs have been subtracted from the economic gross benefits, the issue remains of how to compare costs and benefits occurring in different years. One project may give greater benefits in the early years, while another investment has a longer life. To compare them a discount rate or interest rate is required. The basis for calculating this rate is one of the perennial problems of investment decisions. Is the appropriate rate given by the marginal productivity of capital, the interest rate paid to savers (and if so, which one) or by the consumers' (or planners') time preference (and if so, how does one calculate it)?

Furthermore, investments differ in the extent to which the resulting output is consumed and saved. Saving and reinvestment usually are not desired for their own sake, but for the contribution they make to greater consumption in the future. The effect of each investment on savings and reinvestment, and therefore future consumption, must be incorporated in the criteria for appraising the original investment.

Finally there are various side effects of investments that have to be taken into account, which in some cases may not be side effects at all but crucial to the decision. These include linkage effects, external economies and diseconomies, the effect on regional income and on income distribution, and the effects on population growth, and on attitudes, foreign economic influence and/or domination, and so forth. In approving projects, not all of these issues can be evaluated in each case, nor need they be, since alternative investment projects may not differ significantly in their impact. If two projects are unlikely to make a significant difference to population growth, then the issue of population need not be examined in appraising these projects. In addition many of these broader, more general issues can be examined only in comparing alternative programs, not in examining alternative projects. For instance, two different industrial investments may not significantly affect income distribution, but concentrating investment on either industry or education could have profound effects. In that case it may be best to leave questions of income distribution to a examination of alternative development strategies, and ignore them in considering the alternative industrial investments.

To limit one's effort is essential to the use of investment criteria, as in many other development decisions. If one tries to appraise, to measure, all dimensions of every possible investment project in an economy the result can be only despair, since this is a task beyond even the most effective government. The result may be to give up the task of quantitative appraisal entirely and to fall back on ad hoc judgments and prejudice expressed as judgment. Thus, one of the crucial questions in appraising investments is which criteria are sufficiently important to be worth quantifying.

Suggested Readings on Project Selection (Cases 2, 3, 4)

The student is expected to be familiar with starred (*) items.

Criteria for Project Selection

1. *Tinbergen, Jan. *The Design of Development.* Baltimore: Johns Hopkins Press, 1958.

2. Papanek, Gustav F. "Framing a Development Program." *International Conciliation,* no. 527, March 1960, pp. 307–372.

3. *Alchian, A. A. "The Rate of Interest, Fischer's Rate of Return Over Cost and Keynes' Internal Rate of Return." *American Economic Review,* vol. 45, December 1955, pp. 938–943. Reprinted in: *The Management of Corporate Capital.* Edited by Ezra Solomon. Illinois: The Free Press of Glencoe, 1959, pp. 67–71.

4. *Robinson, Romney. "The Rate of Interest, Fischer's Rate of Return Over Cost and Keynes' Internal Rate of Return: Comment." *American Economic Review,* vol. 46, December 1956, pp. 972–73. Reprinted in: *The Management of Corporate Capital,* pp. 72–73.

5. *Hirschleifer, J. "On the Theory of Optimal Investment Decision." *The Journal of Political Economy,* vol. 66, August 1958, pp. 329–352. Reprinted in: *The Management of Corporate Capital,* pp. 205–228.

6. Chenery, Hollis B. "Development Policies and Programmes." *The Economic Bulletin for Latin America,* vol. 3, March 1958, pp. 51–77.

7. *Eckstein, Otto. "Investment Criteria for Economic Development and the Theory of Intertemporal Welfare Economics." *The Quarterly Journal of Economics,* vol. 71, February 1957, pp. 56–85.

8. *———. "A Survey of the Theory of Public Expenditure Criteria." *Public Needs, Sources and Utilization.* National Bureau of Economic Research. Princeton: Princeton University Press, 1961, pp. 439–504.

9. *Chenery, Hollis B. "Comparative Advantage and Development Policy." *Surveys of Economic Theory,* vol. 2. New York: St. Martin's Press, 1965, pp. 125–137. Also in: *American Economic Review,* vol. 51, March 1961, pp. 18–31.

10. ———. "The Application of Investment Criteria." *The Quarterly Journal of Economics,* vol. 67, February 1953, pp. 76–96.

11. Bruno, Michael. "The Optimal Choice of Import-Substituting and Export Promoting Projects." *Planning the External Sector: Techniques, Problems, and Policies.* New York: United Nations, 1967.

12. *Balassa, Bela, and Schydlowsky, D. M. "Effective Tariffs, the Domestic Cost of Foreign Exchange and the Equilibrium Exchange Rate." *The Journal of Political Economy,* vol. 76, July 1968.

13. Little, I. M. D., and Mirrlees, James A. *Manual of Industrial Project Analysis in Development Countries,* vol. 2. Paris: OECD Development Center, 1969.

Shadow Pricing

14. *Chenery, Hollis B. "Comparative Advantage and Development Policy." *Surveys of Economic Theory,* vol. 2. New York: St. Martin's Press, 1965, pp. 137–146. Also in: *American Economic Review,* vol. 51, March 1961, pp. 31–41.

15. Papanek, Gustav F., and Qureshi, Moeen A. "The Use of Accounting Prices in Planning." *Organization, Planning and Programming for Economic Development.* United States paper prepared for the U.N. Conference on the Application of Science and Technology for the Benefit of the Less Developed Areas. Washington: U.S. Government Printing Office, 1962, pp. 95–105.

16. *Schydlowsky, Daniel M. "On the Choice of a Shadow Price for Foreign Exchange." Harvard University, Center for International Affairs. Economic Development Report No. 108.

17. Bruton, Henry J., and Bose, S. R. *The Pakistan Export Bonus Scheme.* Monographs in the Economics of Development, No. 11. Karachi, Pakistan: The Pakistan Institute of Development Economics, 1963.

18. *Conard, J. W. *An Introduction to the Theory of Interest.* Berkeley: University of California Press, 1959, pp. 1–154.

19. Feldstein, M. S., and Flemming, J. S. "The Problem of Time-Stream Evaluation: Present Values vs. Internal Rate of Return Rules." *Bulletin of the Oxford Institute of Economics and Statistics,* vol. 26, February 1964, pp. 79–85.

20. Feldstein, M. S. "The Social Time Preference Discount Rate in Cost-Benefit Analysis." *Economic Journal,* vol. 74, June 1964, pp. 360–379.

21. Arrow, Kenneth. "Optimal Capital Policy, the Cost of Capital and Myopic Decision Rules." *Annals of the Institute of Statistical Mathematics,* vol. 16 (1964), supplement 3, pp. 21–30.

22. Frisch, Ragnar. "Dynamic Utility." *Econometrica,* vol. 32, July 1964, pp. 418–424.

23. ———. "A Complete Scheme for Computing all Direct and Cross Demand Elasticities in a Model with Many Sectors." *Econometrica,* vol. 27, April 1959, pp. 177–196.

Uncertainty

24. Dorfman, Robert. "Uncertainty." *Design of Water Resource Systems.* Edited by A. Mass, et al. Cambridge: Harvard University Press, 1962, pp. 129–158.

25. Raiffa, Howard. *Decision Analysis: Introductory Lectures on Choices Under Uncertainty.* Reading, Mass.: Addison Wesley, 1969.

26. Magee, J. F. "Decision Trees for Decision Making." *Harvard Business Review,* vol. 42, July and August 1964, pp. 126–138.

27. ———. "How to Use Decision Trees in Capital Investment." *Harvard Business Review,* vol. 42, September and October 1964, pp. 79–96.

Foreign Private Investment

28. Vernon, Raymond. "Foreign-owned Enterprise in Developing Countries." *Public Policy,* vol. 15 (1966), pp. 361–380.

29. ———. "Multinational Enterprise and National Sovereignty." *Harvard Business Review,* vol. 45, March/April 1967, pp. 156–172.

30. ———. "Long-run Trends in Concession Contracts." *Proceedings of American Society of International Law,* vol. 61, April 1967.

31. MacDougall, G. D. A. "The Benefits and Costs of Private Investment from Abroad: A Theoretical Approach." *Economic Record,* vol. 36, March 1960, pp. 13–35.

Country Background: Pakistan

Pakistan gained its independence in 1947 with the surrender of sovereignty by Great Britain over undivided India. The Muslim majority areas were combined to form two noncontiguous areas, East and West Pakistan. Mass migrations and bloodshed accompanied the process of partition and it has been estimated that 6.5 million Muslim refugees came to Pakistan while 5.5 million Hindus and Sikhs emigrated. The exchange of population resulted in an inflow of cultivators and artisans and an outflow of merchants, industrialists, and professionals. Only a few of the civil service elite, which had participated in the British administration of the subcontinent, chose to come to Pakistan.

Of Pakistan's total geographic area of 365,529 square miles, East Pakistan comprises only 15 per cent, although over half of the population resides there.[1] The resultant density of approximately 1,200 persons per square mile makes this region among the most densely inhabited in the world. By contrast, West Pakistan has a relatively low population density of 165 persons per square mile.

The two provinces have distinct geographic characteristics which accentuate their physical separateness. East Pakistan is essentially a low flat deltaic region formed by two of the largest rivers in Asia: the Ganges and the Brahmaputra. It has a typical monsoon climate. The region is subject to periodic flooding by its vast river system. Although flooding is a major factor in maintaining the fertility of the soil, it is often so severe as to be destructive. The river system provides a relatively inexpensive mode of transportation, at the same time it constitutes a serious obstacle to the development of a more modern system of transportation and communication.

West Pakistan, by contrast, lies wholly outside the tropics and its climate is more nearly akin to that of the Middle East than to Southeast Asia. Only the Northern areas receive enough rainfall to permit agriculture without irrigation. The rivers of the Indus basin provide the water resources for the vast irrigation system without which West Pakistan would be largely desert.

Economic Structure and Performance

The general features of the Pakistan economy are broadly similar to those found in many of the less developed countries. With an estimated population of 110 million in 1963/64, Pakistan suffers a high level of unemployment

---

[1] Much of this data is taken from G. F. Papanek, "Economic Survey," in the *Far East and Australasia,* 1969 (London).

18

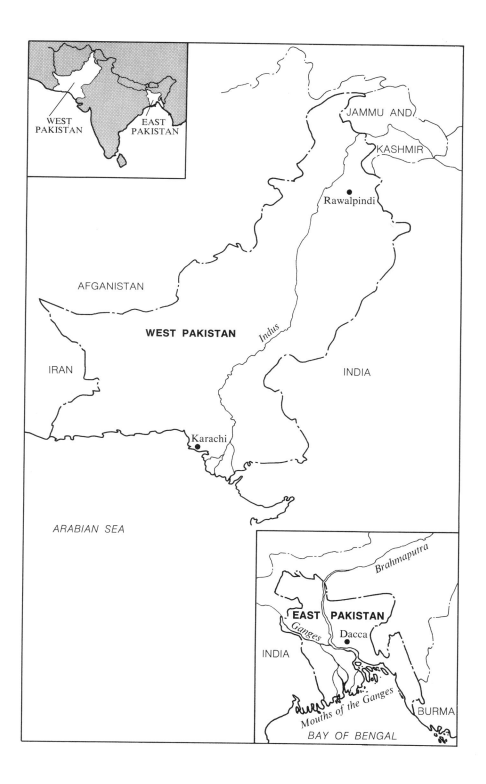

WEST
PAKISTAN

EAST
PAKISTAN

JAMMU AND

KASHMIR

Rawalpindi

AFGANISTAN

WEST PAKISTAN

Indus

IRAN

INDIA

Karachi

ARABIAN SEA

Brahmaputra

EAST PAKISTAN

Ganges

Dacca

INDIA

Mouths of the Ganges

BURMA

BAY OF BENGAL

and underemployment complicated by a high population growth rate, conservatively estimated at 2.8 per cent per year. Unemployment has been estimated as 20 per cent of the labor force. Per capita income was estimated at Rs. 359 ($75 at the official exchange rate), placing Pakistan among the poorest countries of the world.

The economy is dominated by agriculture, which provides nearly half of the gross national product. Less than 15 per cent of the population is classified as urban. Although agricultural output has been growing at well over three per cent per annum since 1959/60, sharp fluctuations in the output level are common, especially in East Pakistan. Large-scale manufacturing[2] contributed about eight per cent to gross national product in 1963/64 and has been the most rapidly growing sector of the economy. Its output still consists largely of textile products and other consumer goods, although the production of capital goods has been rising rapidly. Consequently the economy is forced to import most of its capital goods. In the 1960s nearly one-third of total fixed investment has been financed by foreign aid. Imports of finished consumer goods (including food) have accounted for only one quarter of total imports since the mid-1950s.

Pakistan began its development struggling to overcome the effects of partition. It has few natural resources, except for natural gas, relatively fertile agricultural land, and an underground water supply in West Pakistan. The country lacks important mineral resources.

Despite these unpromising conditions, Pakistan has managed since 1959/60 to achieve one of the highest rates of growth for a mineral-poor less developed country, after a period of stagnation in the 1950s. According to official figures gross national product since independence (1949/50–1963/64) has increased at 3.1 per cent per year and per capita income at 0.7 per cent. In the 1960s (1959/60 to 1963/64) the rate of increase for GNP has reached 5.4 per cent, or over 6.1 per cent according to some unofficial data. In the latter period the rate of increase in agriculture has exceeded the annual increase of population. Whereas prior to 1959/60 the major growth impetus came from the rapidly growing industrial sector, since then both agriculture and industry have contributed to development.

Considerable fluctuations in the level of GNP affected the economy in the 1950s largely as a result of the effect of the weather on agricultural production. However, the adoption of modern agricultural technology during the 1960s, especially in West Pakistan, seems not only to have increased crop production but also to have reduced the effect of the weather.

The structure of the economy has changed. While agriculture continues to be the largest single sector, its share in total GNP has declined and has been less than 50 per cent in 1962/63 and 1963/64. At the same time the share of total manufacturing in GNP has increased from 2 per cent in

---

[2] Large-scale manufacturing refers to firms employing 20 or more persons and using power.

1949/50 to 11 per cent in 1963/64. Large-scale manufacturing, which can be broadly identified with modern industrial activities, now constitutes 70 per cent of total manufacturing.

The pattern of growth in national product is partly the result of changes in investment. Real investment has doubled roughly every five years.[3] The rate of increase in investment, however, has been uneven, rising rapidly prior to 1954/55, slowing down during the First Plan period (1955/56–1959/60) and again increasing sharply during the Second Plan period (1960/61–1964/65). By 1963/64, the ratio of gross investment to GNP had risen to nearly 18 per cent.

The share of the public and private sectors in total fixed investment has undergone considerable change. Prior to 1959/60, the public sector accounted for less than 30 per cent of investment; since then it has risen to over 50 per cent. The shift reflects the commitment of the Government to development, the need to develop an adequate infrastructure and the desire to foster industrial development in East Pakistan, where the private sector has been less active. Despite the shift, private investment has continued to increase at an annual compound rate of over ten per cent since 1959/60.

In the period immediately following independence, domestic savings were low with investment financed largely by drawing down sterling balances accumulated during World War II. By 1954/55, savings as a proportion of GNP were around seven per cent but during the next few years (the First Plan period), the slow rate of growth of national income made it difficult to further increase the saving rate. From 1959/60 to 1963/64, however, the marginal savings rate was high and the average rate became about 12 per cent.

One of the outstanding features of the development process in Pakistan has been the absence of any noticeable inflationary pressure. Over the Second Plan period, when investment increased rapidly, the yearly rates of price increase were between 2.1 and 2.4 per cent. To a considerable extent the government's ability to keep the price level stable, while devoting an increasing share of the national product to nonconsumptive use, was made possible through increased inflows of foreign aid, in particular foodgrain imports under the PL 480 program of the United States and the Government's ability to raise taxes, increasing the revenue available for development.

The Foreign Sector

Like many less developed countries, Pakistan, since the mid-1950s, has earned less from exporting goods and services than its payments for imports—it has had a current account deficit. To compensate for an over-

---

[3] It is necessary to insert a strong caveat here regarding investment and savings data for Pakistan. Neither series has a high degree of reliability and both are subject to frequent revisions in light of new data. While alternative sources and methods of estimation may yield divergent results, the data do reveal a consistent pattern.

valued exchange rate, the government provided special inducements to exports and controlled imports. While maintaining this "disequilibrium system" in the foreign sector, Pakistan has during the 1960s increasingly used indirect measures to allocate imports and to stimulate export earnings.

After the collapse of the raw materials boom following the end of the Korean war, Pakistan faced a serious foreign exchange problem. Demand for imports continued, to meet the demands of the nascent industrial sector for raw materials and intermediate goods, the demand for consumer goods imports from a growing population, especially in the urban sector, and the demand for capital goods for the rapidly expanding investment program. Exports, which consisted primarily of raw jute and cotton, stagnated along with the agricultural sector. The terms of trade for Pakistan had simultaneously deteriorated. About one-third more exports were required to buy the same imports after the middle 1950s than before the Korean boom, and the situation continued to worsen until 1959/60.

By 1954/55 the Government had dealt with the resulting crisis by a severe reduction in imports, accomplished by requiring government licenses before any goods could be brought into the country. Imports had been reduced to only 60 per cent of their level three years earlier. The severest cutbacks were in consumer goods and raw materials for their production, which were reduced to one-quarter of their earlier level. Licensing over time developed into a cumbersome system entailing much bureaucratic interference in private decisions. The system also created monopoly profits for those fortunate enough to obtain import permits. This "scarcity premium" was about 60 per cent of landed cost. In addition, a proclivity for licensing additional industrial capacity even in industries where existing capacity was not fully used, meant that a large number of plants were operating considerably below rated capacity. There were two major reasons for this anomaly. First any expansion of capacity entitled the entrepreneur to additional licenses for imports. At the existing overvalued exchange rate, and given the large license-created monopoly profits on imports, there was a strong incentive for increasing one's claim on imports, even at the cost of expanding plants already underutilized. Second, aid donors preferred to finance specific capital projects and tended to confront Pakistan with the choice of adding to existing plants or reduced assistance.

Since 1959/60 a number of steps have been taken to reduce direct controls and to affect the level and composition of imports through indirect measures. The most innovative and important step was the *export bonus scheme,* inaugurated in January 1959, which affected not only the demand for imports but also the level of exports. One of the main strengths of the scheme is simplicity. Exporters, whose commodities are covered by the scheme, receive a voucher equal to a government-determined proportion of the value of their exports. This voucher can then be freely sold and entitles its owner to purchase foreign exchange at the official exchange rate equivalent to the face value of the voucher. This foreign exchange can then be used to import most goods. Given the scarcity of foreign exchange, bonus vouchers, that is the entitlement alone, usually sell at 150 to 180 per cent of their face value. Since the importer in addition has to buy foreign exchange at the official rate of 4.7 rupees to the dollar the exchange rate facing the importer using bonus vouchers becomes approximately Rs. 12.00 per dollar.

The bonus voucher system is easily understood through a simple equation. Let *Pf* be the price at which a commodity covered by the bonus scheme is sold in the foreign market. If the bonus rate on this commodity is b and the premium for vouchers is *v* then the earnings of the exporter, *Px,* are given by

$$Px = Pf\,(1 + bv).$$

For a commodity with a bonus rate of 30 per cent ($b = .30$) and with a premium on vouchers of 150 per cent of their face value ($v = 1.50$) the rupee earnings of the exporters (Px) are 145 per cent of the price at which the commodity was sold in the foreign market. Importers, who after buying the voucher must still pay for the foreign exchange, would face an exchange rate of 250 per cent of the regular exchange rate.

The scope of the bonus voucher system has steadily expanded in the direction of including most government imports and most raw materials and intermediate products for the private sector. All manufactured exports were covered by the bonus scheme. By 1963, almost half of all exports were under the bonus scheme.

In addition to the bonus voucher scheme, incentives were provided to exporters by other measures such as tax and import duty rebates intended mainly to offset the high cost of imported inputs.

The export promotion policies have been highly successful. Since 1959/60, exports have increased at an annual rate of eight per cent, compared to stagnation earlier. Growth has been accompanied by a major shift in the commodity composition of exports. Until the late 1950s Pakistan exported essentially only raw materials, with raw jute providing almost half, raw cotton almost one quarter of export earnings. By 1963/64 all raw materials had come down from 90 per cent to about 60 per cent, manufacturers had increased from negligible amounts to over 30 per cent of total export earnings. Invisibles also grew rapidly. The more sophisticated exports, excluding jute and cotton manufactures, accounted for nearly ten per cent of the total. This shift in the commodity composition of exports was due both to the growth in manufacturing and the incentives provided to exports.

Development and Development Strategy

In its initial expression of a comprehensive development strategy, Pakistan emphasized both agriculture and industry and placed major reliance on the private sector.

Nevertheless, agriculture grew very slowly during the 1950s. Subsequently, the rate of agricultural growth nearly tripled, agricultural exports expanded rapidly, and there has been a surge in rural private investment, but these developments largely bypassed East Pakistan where the vagaries of weather are among the most severe in the world. The changed situation, especially in West Pakistan, was brought about through a strategy based on the following assumptions: that farmers would respond to economic stimuli; that the government should take steps to create a favorable economic climate for the farmer; and that modern agricultural inputs had to be supplied at the right place and time. In addition Pakistan benefited from the world-wide major advance in agricultural technology, especially in wheat and rice seeds. To implement its incentive/technology strategy, the government established a buffer stock system to stabilize prices for wheat and rice and heavily subsidized modern inputs—fertilizer, pesticides, new seed varieties, and water. The net result was to make a shift to modern technology for agriculture immensely profitable. As a result, Pakistan which was a major foodgrain deficit country, can soon be a large exporter of wheat and rice. Major problems, however, remain. First, the success in introducing new technology and raising production is still largely concentrated in West Pakistan. The new seed varieties are not as yet well adapted to the monsoon agriculture of East Pakistan and the mini-sized nature of the farms in that province makes water control and other modern technology more difficult to adopt. Second, at the present exchange rate and price structure, agricultural exports are not competitive in the world markets.

By any standard, Pakistan has achieved a remarkably high rate of growth for the industrial sector. Although it began from a very small base, the dynamism of the manufacturing sector shows few signs of diminishing. Though most manufacturing is in private hands, government policies created attractive incentives for industrial investment. Severe import restrictions and generous tax concessions created a situation during the early period of industrialization in which yearly profits of 50 to 100 per cent on investment were not unusual. By the end of the 1950s, rates of return had dropped from their astronomical heights, but this has been offset by a decrease in the administrative obstacles facing the industrialists, the development of infrastructure, the growth of financial and other institutions serving the potential investor, and the greater profitability of manufactured exports. Early investment was in the consumer goods industries and other processes with a relatively simple technology. Subsequently, it also involved less traditional lines of production, such as fertilizer, electrical machinery, and other capital goods.

Pakistan's industrialization policy has often been criticized. First, because the major share of industrial investment took place in West Pakistan for a number of reasons. The second criticism was that industrial development was inefficient, sheltered by high tariffs and quantitative restrictions from foreign competition. Undoubtedly a considerable degree of inefficiency did accompany the rapid growth of manufacturing, but the sharp decline in the prices of manufactured goods and the rapid rise in exports indicate that there has been some increase in efficiency.

With respect to both industry and agriculture, East Pakistan has experienced less growth. As a result, the gap between per capita product in the Province and the higher product in West Pakistan has continued to increase since independence. Regional economic disparities are common, especially in large countries, but Pakistan may be unique in two respects: the provinces are physically separate (and culturally distinct) so population movements on a significant scale are out of the question and the less developed province has a majority of the population. The rapid elimination of economic disparity has therefore been enshrined in the constitution and is a political necessity.

Objectives

The Pakistan Planning Commission has realized that investment decisions can only be properly evaluated given society's objectives. In theory, these are supposed to be expressed in an objective function which attaches quantitative weights to each objective. In practice they are rarely stated in such a clear and unambiguous manner that it is possible to derive an objective or social welfare function. Over the years the Pakistan Planning Commission has attempted to clarify the nation's long-run goals. A rapid increase in per capita product or income is clearly the prime objective. Other stated objectives are:

1. To reduce the degree of disparity in per capita income between East and West Pakistan, and at the same time reduce the intra-provincial levels of disparity in per capita income.

2. To provide new job opportunities; that is, a minimum of 5.5 million jobs between 1965 and 1970, thus absorbing the entire increase in the labor force during this period and reducing existing levels of estimated unemployment by over one-third.

3. To strengthen the country's balance of payments and eliminate net inflows of foreign assistance by 1985.

4. To develop basic industries for the manufacture of producer goods so that the requirements of further industrialization can be met mainly from Pakistan's own productive capacity.

5. To continue the spread of modern agricultural technology both to East Pakistan and to those farmers in West Pakistan who have not yet shared in the benefits from past agricultural programs.

6. To arrest the menacing growth of population by taking decisive steps toward population control.

7. To provide better housing, adequate health services, and greater educational opportunities, especially for the lower income groups.

8. To make substantial progress toward achieving certain specific social goals such as diminishing the inequalities in income distribution; reducing the concentration of wealth and economic power; providing a measure of

social security and promoting social and cultural change conducive to accelerated economic expansion.

In evaluating investment decisions, these stated objectives need to be considered although the Planning Commission itself has recognized that some of the objectives may be in conflict or cannot be quantified. Hence they need to be interpreted broadly in any decision making analysis.

Suggested Readings on Pakistan

Starred items (*) are strongly suggested to those not already familiar with the subject matter.

1. Haq, Mahbub ul. *The Strategy of Economic Planning: A Case Study of Pakistan.* New York: Oxford University Press, 1963.

2. *Lewis, Stephen R., Jr. *Economic Policy and Industrial Growth.* New York: George Allen and Unwin, Ltd., 1969.

3. *Papanek, Gustav F. *Pakistan's Development: Social Goals and Private Incentives.* Cambridge: Harvard University Press, 1967.

4. ————. "Economic Survey." *The Far East and Australasia, 1969.* London: Europa Publications, Ltd., 1969, pp. 269–275.

5. Planning Board, Government of Pakistan. *The First Five-Year Plan: 1955–60.* Karachi, Pakistan: Manager of Government Publications, 1957.

6. Planning Commission, Government of Pakistan. *The Second Five-Year Plan: 1960–65.* Karachi, Pakistan: Manager of Government Publications, 1960.

7. ————. *The Third Five-Year Plan, 1965–70.* Karachi, Pakistan: Manager of Government Publications, 1965.

8. ————. *Socio-Economic Objectives of the Fourth Five-Year Plan (1970–75).* Islamabad, Pakistan: Manager of Government Publications, 1968.

Note: Some of these sources present statistical data which differs from the official statistics which follow. This is partly a matter of definition (for example, the attached refer to Gross National Product at Factor Cost, others prefer Gross Domestic Product at Market Prices) and partly a matter of basic data used; nonofficial statistics often use partial reestimates of particular series long before official series are adjusted. Curiously enough the official data generally show a poorer performance than the nonofficial, especially with respect to growth in the National Product and some of its components.

Table Pk-1 Gross National Product of Pakistan at Constant Factor Cost of 1959/60 (Rs. millions)

Year	Agriculture	Manufacturing	All Others	Total	Population (Millions)	GNP/Capita (Rs.)
1949/50	14,669	1,433	8,364	24,466	79	311
1950/51	15,112	1,539	8,722	25,373	81	315
1951/52	14,549	1,645	9,201	25,395	82	308
1952/53	14,917	1,792	9,430	26,139	84	310
1953/54	16,053	1,999	9,724	27,776	86	322
1954/55	15,654	2,220	10,034	27,908	88	316
1955/56	15,135	2,439	10,260	27,834	90	308
1956/57	16,266	2,580	10,651	29,497	92	319
1957/58	16,089	2,691	10,939	29,719	94	315
1958/59	15,923	2,818	11,403	30,144	97	312
1959/60	16,753	2,930	11,756	31,439	99	318
1960/61	17,285	3,262	12,539	33,086	101	326
1961/62	18,183	3,630	13,230	35,043	104	337
1962/63	18,272	3,973	14,039	36,284	107	340
1963/64	19,411	4,351	15,522	39,284	110	359

Source: Government of Pakistan, Central Statistical Office, *Twenty Years of Pakistan in Statistics* (Karachi: Manager of Publications, 1968).

Table Pk–2   *Sectoral Origin of Gross National Product—Pakistan*

Sector	1949/50	1954/55	1959/60	1963/64
Agriculture	60.0%	56.1%	53.3%	49.4%
Manufacturing	5.9	8.0	9.3	11.1
(1) Large-scale	(24.1)	(45.1)	(53.4)	(64.8)
(2) Small-scale	(75.9)	(54.9)	(46.6)	(35.2)
Construction	1.0	1.5	2.1	4.3
Others	33.1	34.4	35.3	35.2
	100.0%	100.0%	100.0%	100.0%

Source: Calculated from: Government of Pakistan, Central Statistical Office, *Twenty Years of Pakistan in Statistics* (Karachi: Manager of Publications, 1968).

Table Pk–3   *Growth Rates for GNP and Major Sectors*[1]
(Per cent per annum)

Sector	1949/50–1963/64	1949/50–1959/60	1959/60–1963/64
1. Agriculture	1.8	1.2	3.5
1a. Major Crops	2.1	1.3	4.0
1b. Other agriculture	1.3	1.1	2.8
2. Manufacturing	7.7	7.6	9.9
2a. Large scale manufacturing[2]	14.2	15.8	14.8
3. All other sectors	3.9	3.3	6.7
4. Total GNP	3.1	2.4	5.4
5. GNP/capita	0.7	[3]	2.8

Source: Calculated from: Government of Pakistan, Central Statistical Office, *Twenty Years of Pakistan in Statistics* (Karachi: Manager of Publications, 1968).
[1] Derived from the least-squares regression log $Y = a + b$ (time) with all values in constant 1959/60 prices.
[2] Large-scale manufacturing activities covers all firms employing 20 or more persons and using power.
[3] Not significantly different from zero.

Table Pk–4   *Expenditure on Gross National Product*
(Rs. millions; current prices)

Item	1959/60	1963/64
1. Consumption	30,550	38,673
(a) Private	27,747	34,134
(b) Public[1]	2,803	4,539
2. Gross fixed investment	3,120	7,385
(a) Government	} 1,610	} 3,945
(b) Semi-government		
(c) Private	1,510	3,440
3. Change in stocks	40	240
4. Exports	2,080	2,785
5. Imports	−3,109	−5,508
6. Expenditure on GNP	32,679	43,475

Source: Calculated from Planning Commission estimates.
[1] Includes current government development expenditures.

Table Pk–5   *Investment and Savings Ratios*
(*Rs. millions; current prices*)

	1954/55	*1959/60*	*1963/64*
Gross investment (I)	2,027	3,840	7,625
Gross savings (S)	1,463	2,875	5,130
GNP (mkt prices)	21,920	32,679	43,575
I/GNP	9.2%	11.8%	17.5%
S/GNP	6.7%	8.8%	11.8%
Marginal savings rate:	13.1%	20.7%	

Source: (1954/55) *Third Five-Year Plan*; (1959/60 and 1964/65) *Final Evaluation of the Second Five-Year Plan.*

Table Pk–6   *Price Indices*

	GNP Implicit Deflator[1]	Wholesale Price Index (Per cent)				
		General	*Food*	*Raw Materials*	*Fuels*	*Manufactures*
1954/55	75.8	—	—	—	—	—
1955/56	81.4	—	—	—	—	—
1956/57	90.2	95.4	93.1	102.6	96.4	99.7
1957/58	95.6	95.6	92.8	103.2	99.2	102.1
1958/59	93.0	93.9	93.4	92.3	101.1	97.0
1959/60	100.0	100.0	100.0	100.0	100.0	100.0
1960/61	105.1	103.0	100.5	119.2	99.2	101.2
1961/62	104.1	105.9	106.6	107.3	98.7	102.1
1962/63	106.5	104.8	104.9	105.1	99.0	104.9
1963/64	105.1	104.6	104.3	105.3	104.5	105.8

Source: Government of Pakistan, Central Statistical Office, *Statistical Bulletin,* various issues.
[1] At factor cost.

Table Pk–7   *Tax Revenues of the Central and Provincial Governments*

	1954/55	*1959/60* (*Rs. millions; current prices*)	*1963/64*
Tax revenues	1,304	2,000	3,441
Total revenues	1,879	2,640	4,752
GNP (mkt. prices)	21,920	32,679	43,575
Average Rate		(Per cent of GNP at market prices)	
Tax revenues	5.9	6.1	7.9
Total revenues	8.6	8.1	10.9
Marginal Rate		(Per cent of GNP at market prices)	
Tax revenues	6.5	13.2	
Total revenues	7.1	19.4	

Source: GNP at factor cost, CSO *Statistical Bulletin*; Indirect taxes, Planning Commission; Tax Revenues and Total Revenues, 1954–1959 Planning Commission, *Third Five-Year Plan*; 1963/64 *Final Evaluation of the Second Five-Year Plan.*

Table Pk–8   *Trade Ratios*

	1954/55	*1959/60*	*1963/64*
		(Rs. millions; current prices)	
Imports of goods (M)	1,558	2,481	4,430
Exports of goods (X)	1,760	1,843	2,299
GNP (mkt. prices)	21,920	32,679	43,575
Average rate	(Per cent of GNP at market prices)		
M/GNP	7.1	7.5	10.1
X/GNP	8.0	5.6	5.3
Marginal rate	(Per cent of GNP at market prices)		
ΔM/ΔGNP		8.4	18.1
ΔX/ΔGNP		0.8	4.2

Sources: GNP 1954/55: *Third Five-Year Plan.* 1959/60–1963/64: *Final Evaluation of the Second Five-Year Plan.* Trade data: *Monthly Statistical Bulletin*, various issues.
Note: Trade figures for 1954/55 were adjusted for devaluation. Invisibles are excluded from all data.

Table Pk–9   *Commodity Import and Exports of Pakistan*

	Imports (1)	*Exports*[a] (2)	*Surplus/Deficit* (3 = 2 − 1)
		(Rs. millions; current prices)	
1951/52	2,237	2,554	+317
1953/54	1,118	1,510	+392
1955/56	1,325	1,784	+459
1957/58	2,050	1,422	−628
1959/60	2,461	1,843	−618
1961/62	3,109	1,843	−1266
1963/64	4,430	2,299	−2131

Source: Government of Pakistan, Central Statistical Office, *Statistical Bulletin*, various issues.
[a] Includes re-exports

Table Pk–10   *Structure of Pakistan's Commodity Exports*

Item	*1951/52*	*1954/55*	*1957/58* (*Per cent*)	*1960/61*	*1963/64*
1. Jute, raw	50.0	51.2	60.1	47.1	32.8
2. Jute, manufactured	—	1.9	6.4	17.5	13.9
3. Cotton, raw	38.7	25.4	15.2	7.7	14.8
4. Cotton, manufactured	—	0.1	2.2	6.5	8.2
5. Hides and skins	1.6	2.4	2.3	3.1	2.2
6. Wool	1.5	4.3	4.7	3.9	3.3
7. Tea	2.1	4.8	1.3	0.1	—
8. Rice	—	1.7	—	2.7	4.6
9. Fish, excluding canned	0.5	2.2	1.4	3.2	4.3
10. Manufactures, nes	—	0.5	1.9	4.0	9.5
11. Others, nes	5.6	5.4	4.5	4.2	6.4
Total	100.0	100.0	100.0	100.0	100.0

Source: Government of Pakistan, Central Statistical Office. *Statistical Bulletin*, various issues.

Table Pk–11   *Structure of Pakistan's Commodity Imports*

	Consumer Goods	Raw Materials for		Capital Goods
		Consumer Goods	Capital Goods	
		(Per cent)		
1951/52	44.2	24.5	22.6	8.7
1953/54	39.2	18.1	28.5	14.1
1955/56	32.6	17.4	36.6	13.4
1957/58	41.8	12.2	33.1	12.9
1959/60	30.8	17.1	37.8	14.4
1961/62	22.3	15.6	47.7	14.5
1963/64	22.1	14.0	48.5	15.3

Source: Nurul Islam, *Imports of Pakistan: Growth and Structure* (Karachi: Pakistan Institute of Development Economics, 1967).
Note: Totals may not add up due to rounding.

Table Pk–12   *Exports under Bonus Vouchers*

	Bonus Voucher Exports	Total Exports	Bonus Voucher Exports as a per cent of total exports
	(Rs. millions)		
1959	552	1527	36.1%
1961	725	1902	38.1%
1963	889	1983	44.9%

Source: Government of Pakistan, Ministry of Finance, *Pakistan Economic Survey*, 1967/68 and *Bulletin of the State Bank of Pakistan.*
Note: Exports as tabulated by the State Bank refer to foreign exchange receipts and will, because of differences in timing, differ from exports as shown in Table Pk-9 which refer to physical movement of goods.

Table Pk–13   *Imports under Bonus Vouchers*

	Bonus Voucher Imports (1)	Total Imports (2)	Bonus Voucher Imports as a per cent of total (3 = 1/2)
	(Rs. millions)		
1959	76	1681	4.5%
1961	155	3056	5.1%
1963	203	4232	4.8%

Composition of Imports under Bonus Vouchers
(Per cent)

	1963
Consumer Goods	23.2
Raw Materials	42.6
Machinery and Spares	34.2
	100.0

Source: (1) Government of Pakistan, Ministry of Finance, *Pakistan Economic Survey*, 1967/68 and (2) *Bulletin of the State Bank.*

Table Pk–14   *Bonus Voucher Quotations*

Year	Yearly Average
1959	162.8
1961	121.4
1963	162.0

Source: Government of Pakistan, Ministry of Finance, *Pakistan Economic Survey* (various issues).

Table Pk–15   *Rates of Taxes on Imported Goods by Type of Commodity*

Type of goods	1959/60	1960/61	1964/65
		(*Per cent of C & F price*)	
1. *Consumption Goods*			
Essentials	35	55	56
Semi-luxuries	54	111	118
Luxuries	99	140	144
2. *Raw Materials for Consumer Goods*			
Unprocessed	26	27	31
Processed	43	50	65
3. *Raw Materials for Capital Goods*			
Unprocessed	23	28	32
Processed	38	40	55
4. *Capital Goods*			
Consumer durables	18	85	91
Machinery and equipment	14	17	22

Source: Ghulam Mohammed Rahdu, "The Rate Structure of Indirect Taxes in Pakistan," *Pakistan Development Review*, vol. 4 (Autumn 1964), pp. 527–551 and "Supplementary Study: Rate Structure of Indirect Taxes in Pakistan: 1963/64 and 1964/65." Unpublished (Karachi: Pakistan Institute of Development Economics, June 1965).

Table Pk–16   *Average QR-Induced Scarcity Premium on Imported Commodities in Pakistan[1] 1964/65*

	East Pakistan	West Pakistan (*Per cent*)	All Pakistan
Consumption Goods	44.2	48.1	47.2
Intermediate Goods	41.5	38.0	40.0
Capital Goods	39.7	40.1	40.0
Total	41.0	43.0	42.5

Source: M. L. Pal as quoted in Alamgir, Mohiuddin, "The Domestic Price of Imported Commodities in Pakistan, A Further Study," *The Pakistan Development Review*, vol. 8 (Spring 1968), pp. 35–73, Table I.
[1] Exclusive of 10–15% "normal" profit.

Case 2: The Social Calculus: Steel Mill or Paper Pulp Plant

In 1964 the Planning Commission of Pakistan is asked to recommend whether a steel mill or a paper pulp plant should be set up during the next five-year plan period. Given the limited resources, particularly foreign exchange, which can be made available for industrial development, it is not possible to develop both plants. The total cost of the steel mill ($136.5 million) is considerably greater than the total cost required to build the paper pulp plant ($38.5 million). However, the Planning Commission is assured by the Ministry of Finance that total allocable resources are just sufficient to build the steel mill. If the paper pulp plant is the preferred investment, the Planning Commission will allocate the unused capital to the execution of projects in its portfolio with benefits at *least* as great as the paper pulp plant.

Both steel and pulp are presently being imported. The proposed steel mill will substitute domestic production for much, but not all, of the presently imported steel. It will therefore not face a marketing problem. The pulp plant, in contrast, will need to export a considerable part of its output, but it will be able to do so only if its prices are internationally competitive. Either plant might be in private hands, or in the absence of private interest, will be developed by a government industrial development corporation. Management for either plant can therefore be made available. The Planning Commission has to advise which of the two plants will make the greater contribution to the nation's development objectives.

Project reports are available for both projects, containing much engineering data but considerably less economic information. Important economic information on the two projects is abstracted in Tables 2–1A and 2–1B.

Financing

The Planning Commission assumes, quite realistically, that total resources for investment, both savings and foreign exchange, are given. These resources include Pakistan's own and those provided through foreign loans and grants. In other words, the foreign resources made available for one project can, if that project is not executed, be shifted to other projects in the plan.

Risk and Uncertainty

As a basis for appraising risk and uncertainty, price series for the products, steel and pulp, were obtained. (Assume the two plants would come into operation in 1966.) These are given in Table 2–2.

Factor Costs

In addition to the data contained in the project reports, the Planning Commission considered it necessary to obtain information on the appropriate prices to use for various factors of production. The data furnished in the project proposals assumed, of course, market prices. The Commission's staff is well aware of the arguments for the use of "accounting" or "shadow" prices. Some of the relevant information is given in Tables 2–3A and 2–3B. Other factors will also bear on the question of whether accounting prices should be used, and, if so, how to calculate them.

Some Arguments

In examining the two proposals, the Planning Commission has before it arguments on building a steel mill from a previous discussion of such a project. Some of the most important of these arguments are given below:

"As anticipated, experts of the Planning [Commission] have reviewed this project from a highly theoretical and unworkable standard and completely detached from any practical aspects or the actual conditions as prevailing in Pakistan.

"It has never been claimed that the iron and steel project as visualised and as worked out by our technical advisers would, at any stage and on paper, be remunerative on the same level as some other projects. . . ."

"Any country that is striving towards its industrialisation has to have two objectives:

1. To set up industries that are economically remunerative and where the investments yield a good return and for which there is either an internal or an external market. In brief industries that would be large scale earners.

2. Secondly, there is a second group of industries which come under the category of essential, though not giving high returns in themselves, and strategic. The existence of these industries is of vital importance to the country and without which industries coming under Group I cannot flourish. The jute industry and the iron and steel industry come under this category.

"In the case of the iron and steel industry, although it is not a commodity to be exported, the industry in itself is of a nature which affects the very core of our economy and future development. We have set up ordnance factories involving an enormous outlay. These factories are at present entirely dependent on the import of steel from abroad. We have a fairly large capacity in rolling mills in the country. These mills have been working in a spasmodic manner and at high operating costs merely on account of the non-availability at different periods of raw material in the form of ingots and billets.

"Had the experts of the Planning [Commission] studied in detail the economic conditions through which the country has passed in the last 8 years, they would have found that we have been through some extreme cycles of depression merely on account of lack of steel. In spite of a very substantial increase in the world production of steel, to us supplies have been erratic and irregular either due to non-availability or due to a shortage of foreign exchange.

"And it is a self-evident truth no country in the world would like to export iron and steel in raw or semi-finished form to any other country. The object is to secure full conversion in the country of origin. The difference in the price quoted for ingots and billets as against the price of finished goods amply proves this. We have been through an extreme shortage of steel in the beginning of 1948–49, again repeated in 1950 and we were going again through that serious situation *today*.

"In their economic appraisal of the project the experts of the Planning [Commission] have adopted a novel procedure, i.e. giving the foreign exchange a new valuation altogether. Were we to apply this standard from the very beginning, I am confident that no industry could have been developed in Pakistan and the first industry to suffer would have been the cotton textiles.

"This iron and steel industry is of the utmost strategic importance, and it would be extremely difficult to give this any money value as the effect is far-reaching. The industry must come and without which we cannot exist. But with all this the industry will not be a dead loss. Applying common standards it will pay its way. The profits will not be large and were never claimed to be so, but it is definite that there would be a return in keeping with normal standards, i.e., 5–7%. If an industry, which is set up for strategic purposes, can give this yield, nothing more is needed.

"In brief, the whole premises on which the experts' case has been built up is wrong and the best way to realise the importance of this industry and its strategic nature is to calculate as to what would be the effect on the economy of the country when steel is not obtainable and which happens to be the present position."

The Question

The Planning Commission needs to decide whether to recommend the steel plant *or* the paper pulp mill. It needs to justify the criterion, or criteria, employed, the prices used to calculate costs and benefits, and the nature of the calculations made. It should take account of risk and uncertainty in its recommendations. However, in view of the similarity in gestation periods and length of life of the projects, discounting of future costs and benefits can be dispensed with. In addition, savings and reinvestment as a proportion of the increased production are likely to be similar for the two projects; thus savings/reinvestment effects can be ignored.

The explanation should obviously be understandable to the Cabinet Members and others concerned with the decision, most of whom are not well versed in theoretical economics. Furthermore, the Planning Commission's analysis must respond to the arguments presented in the above quoted article which has received widespread publicity in the national press.

Table 2–1A   *Steel Plant Project*

			Amount
A. *Total Investment*			*(Million US Dollars)*
1. Total cost of project			$136.50
of which rupee costs are			38.00
2. Capital Structure			
Equity			50.00
Debt (Foreign)			86.50
		Total	$136.50

B. Output and Sales

Product	Quantity (tons/annum)	Selling Price (Rs./ton)	Revenue (Rs. millions/Annum)
1. Billets	100,000	520.00	52.00
2. Sections	50,000	850.00	42.50
3. Rails	30,000	900.00	27.00
4. Black sheet	65,000	1,200.00	78.00
5. Galvanized sheet	20,000	1,300.00	26.00
6. Tube strip	50,000	870.00	43.50
7. Tin plate	35,000	1,530.00	53.55
Total	350,000		322.55

Average selling price   Rs. 921.57/ton
Price of equivalent imports
    CIF Karachi   Rs. 823.90/ton

	Amount
C. *Costs*	*(Rs/ton)*
1. Labor, Raw materials, etc.	578.70
2. Depreciation	85.84
3. Management consulting services and supervision	33.93
4. Interest (at 6% per annum)	72.56
Total	771.03

	Amount
Details of costs of labor, raw material, etc. are as follows:	*(Rs/ton)*
1. Labor:	
a. Administrative; maintenance; quality control; etc. (largely skilled)	91.20
b. Production (largely unskilled and semi-skilled)	6.50
	97.71
2. Raw Materials:	
a. Imported—dollar cost	351.82
—Rs. cost, customs, transport, etc.	50.45
	402.27

Table 2–1A **(continued)**

		Amount (Rs/ton)
b.	Domestic	
	Raw materials (lime, dolomite, etc.)	10.07
	Fuels: natural gas	48.31
	fuel oil	8.17
	Water, acetylene, oxygen	6.18
		72.73
3.	Rent and insurance	5.99
	Total costs	578.70

D. *Planned composition of labor force:*

Type	No. of Persons
1. Pakistani management and senior technicians	58
2. Pakistani administrative and clerical employees	409
3. Pakistani skilled and semi-skilled labor	1151
4. Pakistani unskilled and semi-skilled labor	1318
	2936
U.S. technicians: declining from an initial level of	62

Table 2–1B *Paper Pulp Project*

A.	Total Investment	Amount (Rs. millions)
1.	Foreign currency	Rs. 118.432
2.	Local currency	64.947
	Total	Rs. 183.379

B. *Output and Sales*

1. Product	Destination	Quantity (tons/annum)	Price (Rs/ton)	Revenue (Rs. millions/Annum)
a. Pulp	Domestic	18,000	960.00	17.280
b. Pulp	Foreign	54,000	774.00	41.796
Total		72,000		59.076

Average selling price: Rs. 848.00/ton

	(Rs/ton)
2. Export price	
Price FOB Chittagong Port	516.00
Export bonus (subsidy)	258.00
Sub-total	774.00
Less: Transportation, etc. from mill to FOB Chittagong Port	10.00
Total (net)	Rs. 764.00

Table 2–1B **(continued)**

			(*Rs/ton*)	
3.	Domestic price		960.00	
	Less: Transportation, etc. to			
	FOR Chittagong Port		7.00	
				Rs. 953.00
4.	CIF price of import pulp			Rs. 731.00
C.	***Costs***		*Rs./ton*	
1.	Cost of sales:			
	a.	Foreign currency	94.49	
	b.	Domestic currency	418.28	
				512.77
2.	Depreciation:			
	a.	Foreign currency investment	154.50	
	b.	Domestic currency investment	84.90	
				239.40
3.	Interest:			
	a.	Foreign currency (7% per annum)	56.90	
	b.	Domestic currency (5% per annum)	7.20	
				64.10
				Rs. 816.27

Details of costs are as follows:

1.	Labor:			
	a.	Foreign currency	34.31	
	b.	Domestic currency (unskilled labor)	27.13	
				61.44
2.	Raw materials:			
	a.	Bamboo: Foreign currency (depreciation on		
		imported tools and equipment)	12.62	
		Domestic currency:		
		Unskilled labor	257.13	
		Rent, royalties to land owners	24.78	
				294.53
	b.	Chemicals:		
		Foreign currency	47.71	
		Domestic currency	33.64	
				81.35
	c.	Other current inputs:		
		Foreign currency	25.00	
		Domestic currency	88.89	
				113.89
		Sub-total		551.21
		Less: Sale of by-products		
		Caustic soda		38.44
		Total		512.77

Table 2–2 *Price of Steel and Pulp*

Commodity	Country	1956	1957	1958	1959	1960	1961	1962	1963
				Prices (US Dollars/long ton)					
Steel:	Japan	189.00	191.00	116.00	119.00	124.00	120.00	115.00	113.00
	U. K.	145.30	161.80	134.12	117.90	116.75	116.50	116.50	116.50
	U. S.	113.60	122.10	127.00	129.00	128.80	120.51	120.51	121.85
Pulp:	U. S.	n.a.	n.a.	175.85	175.85	174.75	165.75	156.80	155.70

n.a.: not available

Table 2–3A *Information Relating to Factor Costs: Foreign Exchange*

1. Official rate of exchange: Rs. 4.75 = $1.00
2. Free (black) market rate (Switzerland) Rs. 6.50 − 7.50 = $1.00
3. Customs receipts and total imports

Year	Imports[a] (Rs. millions)	Import Duty plus Sales Tax on Imports[b]
1955/56	1,325.1	546.3
1956/57	2,334.6	533.1
1957/58	2,049.9	551.3
1958/59	1,578.4	508.6
1959/60	2,461.0	549.1
1960/61	3,187.6	782.6
1961/62	3,109.1	913.1
1962/63	3,818.8	1052.0
1963/64	4,430.2	1173.2

Sources: [ac]Government of Pakistan, Central Statistical Office, *Monthly Statistical Bulletin*, May 1968, vol. 16 no. 5 (Karachi: Manager of Publications).
[b] Government of Pakistan, Central Board of Revenue, Statistical Office, Rawalpindi (unpublished data).
Note: From 1952/53 on there were severe restrictions on imports. For an evaluation of these see (3) in the Suggested Readings, p. 40 (a summary is given in Table Pk.-16). In addition, the Government of Pakistan operates an "export bonus" scheme, which is in effect a subsidy on exports. For a description and analysis of this scheme, see (1), (2) and (4) in the Suggested Readings, p. 40 (as well as the introductory section on Pakistan)

Table 2–3B *Information Relating to Factor Costs: Labor*

1. Wage rate for unskilled workers
   a. Casual labor   Rs. 1.50—2.00/day
   b. Factory labor   Rs. 2.00—3.50/day
                                     plus 34% fringe benefits
2. Wage rate for semi-skilled workers   Rs. 3.00—4.50/day
                                     plus 30% fringe benefits

Table 2–3B **(continued)**

3. Estimate of unemployment and underemployment

| | *Labor Force and Employment: 1950–70 (Million man-years)* | | | | |
	1950/51	*1954/55*	*1960/61*	*1964/65*	*1969/70*
Total employment	21.70	23.55	26.15	29.70	35.20
Unemployment	5.60	6.55	7.55	7.55	6.25
Labor force (total)	27.30	30.10	33.70	37.25	41.45
Unemployment as % of total labor force	20.5	21.8	22.4	20.3	15.1

Source: Government of Pakistan, Planning Commission, *The Third Five-Year Plan*, Karachi: Manager of Government Publications, 1965

Suggested Readings

1. Bruton, Henry J., and Bose, Swadesh R. *The Pakistan Export Bonus Scheme.* Karachi, Pakistan: Institute of Development Economics, 1963. (Monographs in the Economics of Development, No. 11.)

2. Mallon, Richard D. "Export Policy in Pakistan." *Pakistan Development Review,* vol. 6, Spring 1966, pp. 57–79.

3. Pal, Mati Lal. "The Determinants of the Domestic Prices of Imports." *Pakistan Development Review,* vol. 4, Winter 1964, pp. 597–621.

4. Soligo, Ronald and Stern, Joseph J. "Some Comments on the Export Bonus, Export Promotion and Investment Criteria." *Pakistan Development Review,* vol. 6, Spring 1966, pp. 38–56.

Case 3: Social Time Preference and External Economies: Multipurpose Project vs. Industrial Investment

A very large multipurpose project, the Tarbela Dam Project, is being proposed for inclusion in Pakistan's Third Five-Year Plan, 1965–1970. The resources that will be required for the Tarbela project would entail cutting back development expenditures in other fields, especially in industry. If Tarbela is to be included in the plan, it will be necessary to eliminate a number of industrial projects, of which the steel mill and paper pulp plant examined in Case 2, can be taken as typical. On the other hand, if Tarbela were deferred, such a cut-back would not be required.

The industrial program or Tarbela will be financed from an identical combination of foreign and domestic resources. Information typical of the industrial alternatives is presented in Case 2. Some relevant information, taken from a series of studies on Tarbela, is given below.

Costs

Table 3–1 shows a breakdown of the cost for Tarbela Dam, exclusive of transmission facilities. Construction will be spread over a nine-year period, with equal annual expenditures.

The major drawback of Tarbela is that the useful life of the reservoir will be rather short because of rapid sedimentation. However its location will allow diversion of water, by gravity flow, to side valley reservoirs in which sedimentation would then take place very slowly. Thus as Tarbela's storage capacity becomes depleted, its value as a source of power generation would increase and its storage for irrigation supplies could be replaced by a side valley reservoir. The construction of a side storage reservoir has been proposed for Gariala. It would have a total cost of $569 million and a foreign exchange component of $359 million. The Gariala project needs to be added to Tarbela proper for the purpose of project appraisal.[1] The combined life of the Tarbela-Gariala project would be fifty years.

Power Benefits

The estimated demand for electric power, at present prices, is shown in Table 3–2 for much of the useful life of Tarbela. These requirements can be met either by Tarbela or by thermal power plants. Table 3–3 shows the required installed generating capacity for the two alternatives.

The Tarbela alternative calls for greater average installed capacity because the water release from the dam is governed, in part, by agricultural needs. This produces large fluctuations in the level of the reservoir during

---

[1] Construction of the Gariala dam, in fact, will take place after Tarbela dam has been completed. However for the present purpose of analysis we can assume that construction would be concurrent.

the course of each year, and substantial "excess capacity" is available during part of the year. The thermal alternative uses gas from the Mari gas fields, allowing for a more even level of operation.

The estimated costs of these two alternatives are shown in Tables 3–4 and 3–5. The headings on the tables are to be interpreted as follows:

1. *Capital Cost:*

a. *Hydro-Thermal and Transmission:* This column shows the capital cost of the operating equipment and transmission lines by year of installation, that is, in the case of the Tarbela program it *includes* the cost of the power units but *excludes* the cost of the dam itself.

b. *Hydro-Capacity Credits:* These figures represent the value of increased generating capacity becoming available as the main dam at Tarbela silts up. This results from the fact that as the main dam silts up, water can be released in an optimal pattern for hydro-electricity generation without having to take account of water requirements for agriculture. The value of this increased capacity is taken by the consultants to be equal to the cost of a 250 MW (megawatt) steam plant.

2. *Operation and Maintenance Costs:*

a. *Hydro-Thermal and Transmission:* Consists of the cost of operating and maintaining the plants and the necessary transmission facilities. It also includes the cost of increases in the transmission facilities at the dates on which these are required (really a capital item).

b. *Hydro-Transfers:* This represents the value of electricity sold to the Southern grid at times when water availability generates excess supply of power on the Northern grid. The value of this power is taken, by the consultants, to be $0.005 per kwh. The amount of electricity expected to be sold represents only part of the excess power available. However the consultants have not made an estimate of the total excess power likely to be available.

3. *Fuel Costs:* Represents the fuel cost for the entire system resulting from cost-minimizing scheduling.

4. *Total Foreign Exchange Cost:* The total foreign exchange component of the previous items (1–3).

The power generated can be used to run tubewells. It has been estimated that it takes 9.3 kwh to operate one tubewell for one hour, and a tubewell running for one hour delivers one acre-inch of water. Tubewells, in addition to providing drainage, can be operated to provide seasonal supplements to Tarbela gravity irrigation. In order to simplify the calculations, it may be assumed that the marginal productivity value of water, on a 12.5 acre farm, considering all the relevant interactions, seasonalities, and constraints, is as given in Table 3–6 and that the cost of transmission to the well-head is between 3 and 6 Rs/kwh. There are approximately 12.5 million acres on which tubewell water could be used.

Agricultural Benefits

Benefits accruing in agriculture would be the additional output due to the increased supply of water through gravity irrigation from Tarbela. The consultants estimated these benefits as follows. An estimate of agricultural output for 1974, the last year of production without Tarbela, was derived. Then projections of the increase in output that would take place, independent of Tarbela, were compared to the estimates of output with Tarbela. The benefits attributable to Tarbela were taken as the difference between the two sets of figures. It was obvious that the results would depend on the assumptions made regarding the increases of other inputs into agriculture. Three alternative assumptions were considered:

1. *Low level of supporting inputs:* A continuation of the present level of supporting agricultural inputs allowing for a normal rate of progress. That is, no special priority would be given to the Tarbela commanded area in the allocation of resources.

2. *Moderate level of supporting inputs:* Some degree of priority in the allocation of resources, at least in the early years, would be given to Tarbela commanded areas. This implies that those areas where Tarbela water would be available would reach a level of inputs which the Indus plain as a whole would only achieve after a number of years.

3. *High level of supporting inputs:* A high priority in the allocation of resources would be given to Tarbela commanded areas. The assumed level of inputs, approaching an optimum, could only be achieved with a great concentration of effort.

The increased value of agricultural production due to Tarbela, under the three alternative assumptions, is given on both a "gross" and "net" return basis in Table 3–7. The "net" return reflects the fact that to achieve the full benefits from Tarbela water, the cultivators have to incur additional cash outlays. Subtracting these cash outlays from "gross" returns yields the estimated "net" returns. A breakdown of these additional cash outlays, on a per acre basis is given in Table 3–8A. Note that the value of family farm labor is not included as a cost and that the amount of such labor is unknown.

Table 3–8B shows the present and projected crop distribution in the Tarbela area. Among the major export items of West Pakistan are raw cotton and cotton textiles. Some sugar and wheat are imported. The real economic cost to Pakistan of most imported wheat is small, since it is provided under the U. S. P. L. 480 (surplus disposal) program. Other crops to be produced in the Tarbela area are neither imported nor exported.

Indirect Benefits

If "full employment" for an agricultural laborer is defined as working for 200 days per year, the employment effect of Tarbela is large. Hired labor alone is estimated to increase as follows:

	Input Assumption	*Additional hired labor*
1.	Low level	200,000 workers
2.	Medium level	275,000 workers
3.	High level	575,000 workers

Data on savings and reinvestment are sketchy and of doubtful accuracy. On the whole, cultivators seem to save about three per cent of their income. Their marginal rate of savings, however, may be substantially higher, though no one knows for sure. Workers' savings rates have been variously estimated at between zero and eight per cent. There is some evidence, of dubious accuracy, that it averages around four per cent. The savings rates out of industrial returns are quite high, and perhaps as much as two-thirds of industrialists earnings, after taxes, are saved and reinvested. For a more detailed analysis of the savings in Pakistan, see (*1*) and (*3*) in the Suggested Readings.

Interest Costs

To make a comparison of the two alternatives, use of a discount rate is clearly called for. Information on the market cost of capital, and on its yield, is sparse and poor. Interest rates charged by commercial banks on certain favored stocks is 6 per cent; on real estate and machinery, it has gone as high as 12 per cent, the legal limit. Treasury bills earn 3–4 per cent and loans to small industrial units are charged 12 to 24 per cent per year. The various international agencies provide loans to Pakistan at a rate of 1.5 to 4.5 per cent per annum.

As regards the capital requirements for various sectors see (*2*) and (*4*) in the Suggested Readings, p. 49.

The Issue to be Resolved

The Planning Commission has to make a recommendation on whether Tarbela should be included in the plan.

In reaching a decision the following questions have to be dealt with:

1. How should the power output of Tarbela be valued, keeping in mind the excess of supply over projected demand at present prices?

2. How should the increased agricultural output from Tarbela Dam water be valued in view of:
   a. uncertainty about the additional production as a result of Tarbela;
   b. difficulties in valuing the different crops produced;
   c. difficulties in costing the additional inputs; and
   d. the employment effects of Tarbela.

3. What discount rate should be used in summing costs spread over nine years and benefits over 50 years?

4. How should the external economies and diseconomies of the two alternatives be valued?

5. Will the two alternative investment programs have different effects

on domestic savings? If so, how can the differential effect on savings be measured and should such difference be reflected in the investment choice?

The Planning Commission is not concerned with exact calculations but rather requires some rough orders of magnitudes in comparing the two alternative programs.

Table 3–1   Tarbela Dam Cost Estimates (Millions of dollars)

Item	Total	Foreign Exchange
1. Pre-contract costs	$ 16.5	$ 4.7
2. Net contract costs	414.4	284.0
3. Contingencies (20% of item 2)	86.2	57.7
4. Engineering administration	36.2	30.0
5. Insurance and miscellaneous costs	9.0	9.0
6. Performance bond	4.0	4.0
7. Land acquisition and resettlement	59.0	—
Sub-total waterworks cost	625.3	389.4
8. Initial power units	113.7	84.2
9. Final power units	56.9	42.9
Sub-total	795.9	516.5
10. Taxes	133.4	—
Total	$929.3	516.5

Table 3–2   Projected Future Power Requirements (Millions of Kwh.)

Year	Non-Agriculture	Tubewells			Grand Total
		Private	Reclamation	Total	
1965	1,519	345	137	482	2,001
1970	2,284	930	685	1,615	3,889
1975	3,757	1,420	1,300	2,720	6,477
1980	5,660	1,560	1,850	3,410	9,070
1985	8,146	1,340	2,350	3,690	11,836
⋮	⋮	⋮	⋮	⋮	⋮
2000	26,106	965	3,450	4,415	30,521

Table 3–3   Alternative Power Capacities (Megawatts)[1]

	Tarbela	Thermal
Existing	497	497
Additional: 1965–75	1,655	1,655
1975–85	2,242	1,316
Installed 1985	4,394	3,468

[1] One Megawatt of installed capacity running at 100% of rated capacity for 1 hour produces 1000 kwh.

Table 3—4 *Power Cost—Tarbela Program* (Rs. millions)

Year	Capital Cost		Operation and Maintenance			Total
	Hydro-Thermal and Transmission	*Hydro-Capacity Credits*	*Hydro-Thermal and Transmission*	*Hydro-Transfers*	*Fuel Cost*	*Foreign Exchange*
1970	3	—	—	—	—	2
1971	63	—	—	—	—	43
1972	39	—	—	—	—	27
1973	55	—	6	16	24	40
1974	84	—	6	16	29	66
1975	77	—	15	19	26	58
1976	95	—	15	22	27	72
1977	103	—	16	23	27	77
1978	116	—	16	23	25	86
1979	119	—	17	29	22	88
1980	113	—	17	33	18	81
1981	172	—	18	33	13	146
1982	74	—	20	35	13	58
1983	14	—	21	35	13	12
1984	30	—	22	35	14	24
1985	—	—	23	35	16	1
1986	—	—	23	35	16	—
1987	—	—	23	34	17	—
1988	—	—	24	33	16	—
1989	—	—	23	32	16	—
1990	—	—	23	31	17	—
1991	—	—	23	31	16	—
1992	—	—	24	25	16	—
1993	—	—	23	21	17	—
1994	—	—	23	16	16	—
1995	—	—	23	11	16	—
1996	—	—	24	6	17	—
1997	—	—	23	3	16	—
1998	—	17	23	—	16	—
1999	—	18	23	—	17	—
2000	—	17	24	—	16	—
2001	—	18	23	—	16	—
2002	—	17	23	—	17	—
2003	—	18	23	—	16	—
2004	—	17	24	—	16	—
2005	—	18	23	—	17	—
2006	—	17	23	—	16	—
2007	—	18	23	—	16	—
2008	—	17	24	—	17	—
2009	—	18	23	—	16	—
2010	—	17	23	—	16	—
2011	—	18	23	—	16	—
2012	—	17	24	—	16	—
2013	—	18	23	—	16	—
2014	4	17	23	—	17	2
2015	17	18	23	—	16	—
Total	1178	315	909	623	757	881

Table 3–5 Power Costs—Thermal Generation Program (Rs. millions)

| | Capital Cost | | Operation and Maintenance | | | Total |
| | Hydro-Thermal | Hydro-Capacity | Hydro-Thermal | Hydro- | Fuel | Foreign |
Year	and Transmission	Credits	and Transmission	Transfers	Cost	Exchange
1970	—	—	—	—	—	—
1971	—	—	—	—	—	—
1972	—	—	—	—	—	—
1973	26	—	4	—	25	18
1974	160	—	4	—	29	98
1975	339	—	7	14	29	235
1976	305	—	9	14	33	217
1977	137	—	11	19	27	86
1978	160	—	12	19	29	117
1979	124	—	13	19	31	92
1980	82	—	13	17	36	61
1981	136	—	15	17	31	123
1982	49	—	16	17	31	38
1983	109	—	17	15	35	103
1984	20	—	18	14	36	21
1985	—	—	19	7	45	5
1986	—	—	19	6	45	—
1987	—	—	19	5	45	—
1988	—	—	19	5	45	—
1989	—	—	19	4	45	—
1990	—	—	19	2	45	—
1991	—	—	19	—	45	—
1992	—	—	19	—	45	—
1993	—	—	19	—	45	—
1994	—	—	19	—	45	—
1995	—	—	19	—	45	—
1996	—	—	19	—	45	—
1997	—	—	19	—	45	—
1998	—	—	19	—	45	—
1999	—	—	19	—	45	—
2000	—	—	19	—	45	—
2001	—	—	19	—	45	—
2002	—	—	19	—	45	—
2003	—	—	19	—	45	—
2004	—	—	19	—	45	—
2005	—	—	19	—	45	—
2006	—	—	19	—	45	—
2007	—	—	19	—	45	—
2008	4	—	19	—	45	—
2009	22	—	19	—	45	—
2010	86	—	19	—	45	—
2011	81	—	19	—	45	—
2012	14	—	19	—	45	—
2013	—	—	19	—	45	—
2014	5	—	19	—	45	—
2015	25	—	19	—	45	—
Total	1884		728	194	1767	1214

Table 3–6 *Marginal Productivity Value of Water*

	Additional Pumping Capacity (acre-inch)	Marginal Productivity Value of Water (Rs./acre-inch)
First	127	Rs. 9.49
Next	49	6.70
Next	52	5.97
Next	42	5.13
Next	142	4.73
Next	52	3.50
Next	41	2.83

Source: Carl H. Gotsch, "Technological Change and Private Investment in Agriculture: A Case Study of the Pakistan Punjab." (Ph.D. thesis, Harvard University, September 1966) p. 89.

Table 3–7 *Gross and Net Agricultural Benefits Attributable to Tarbela (Rs. millions)*

Attributable Increment:	1975	1978	1984	1989	2027	Total 1975–2027
A. Low Input Level						
Gross	346.8	403.8	489.3	513.0	669.8	29,312.3
Net	204.3	232.8	280.3	299.3	437.0	18,073.8
B. Moderate Input Level						
Gross	365.8	465.5	641.3	707.8	1225.5	45,319.8
Net	218.5	294.5	380.0	422.8	736.3	27,288.8
C. High Input Level						
Gross	422.8	627.0	864.5	921.5	1353.8	54,577.5
Net	256.5	408.5	570.0	598.5	798.0	33,867.5

Table 3–8A *Estimated Increase in On-Farm Costs (Rs./Cropped Acre)*

Item		1975			2024		
		Low	Medium	High	Low	Medium	High
1.	Hired labor	20.0	23.0	23.0	40.0	50.0	54.0
2.	Animal traction	43.1	41.9	39.6	14.1	5.3	5.6
3.	Seeds	11.0	12.1	12.4	20.0	25.0	30.0
4.	Fertilizer	11.2	11.9	16.0	35.0	77.5	92.8
5.	Plant protection	1.6	2.0	2.4	5.0	10.0	15.0
6.	Equipment	13.1	13.8	16.7	38.3	76.3	76.3
7.	Packing	1.3	1.4	1.6	3.0	5.0	5.0
8.	Water charges	7.9	7.9	7.9	7.9	7.9	7.9
9.	Taxes	9.5	10.3	10.3	13.0	21.5	24.0
10.	Interest	2.3	2.4	2.6	4.6	7.5	8.4
11.	Others	6.0	5.3	4.5	7.1	8.0	10.0
	Total	127.0	132.0	137.0	188.0	294.0	329.0

Table 3–8B   *Crop Distribution of Additional Output in Tarbela Commanded Area*
(*Per cent of market value of output*)

Crop	Share of Increase
1. Wheat	23.8%
2. Maize	9.7
3. Cotton	−31.7
4. Fodder	5.2
5. Grain	9.9
6. Sugar	70.5
7. Fruits, vegetables	12.6
Total	100.0

Suggested Readings

1. Bergan, Asbjørn. "Personal Income Distribution and Personal Savings in Pakistan: 1963/64." *Pakistan Development Review,* vol. 7, no. 2, Summer 1967, pp. 160–212.

2. Khan, Azizur Rahman, and MacEwan, Arthur. "A Multisectoral Analysis of Capital Requirements for Development Planning in Pakistan." *Pakistan Development Review,* vol. 7, no. 4, Winter 1967, pp. 445–479.

3. Papanek, Gustav F. *Pakistan's Development: Social Goals and Private Incentives.* Cambridge: Harvard University Press, 1967, chapter VII.

4. ———. "Industrial Production and Investment in Pakistan." *Pakistan Development Review,* vol. 4, no. 3, Autumn 1964, pp. 462–490.

Case 4: Foreign Private Investment: The Toquepala Mine

Peru adopted new mining legislation in 1950 with the purpose of strongly promoting the expansion of the mining sector. To this end, the new Code authorized the granting of a number of tax exemptions at the Government's discretion.

The new legislation combined with the high raw material prices resulting from the Korean War Boom resulted in a number of new mining ventures; the most important of these was the proposal to exploit copper deposits at Toquepala.

In early 1953 American Smelting and Refining Company (A.S. & R.) proposed to the Peruvian government that the company be permitted to open a large copper mine situated at Toquepala in the middle of the desert at the Southern end of Peru. In order to operate the mine, A.S. & R., would have to build two complete towns to house its labor force, build a railroad to bring the copper to the port of Ilo, and improve the port of Ilo itself, in addition to the installations connected directly with the mining and smelting of the ore.

The total investment was calculated at U.S. $168 million, broken down as shown in Table 4–1.

These funds would come in part from an equity purchase by A.S. & R. equal to $48.0 million and from local credit lines of Soles 5.0 million ($333,000). The remainder was to be provided through an Export-Import Bank loan, repayable in twenty-five years at five per cent interest, with repayment to start at the end of a six-year grace period, equal to the construction period.

Table 4–2 shows the projected expenditure of funds (excluding import duties) and Table 4–3 shows expected output volumes and operating costs.

The price of refined copper for the life of the mine was estimated to average between 18 and 24 cents per pound. The company based its calculation on 18 cents per pound, the Peruvian planners inclined toward 20 cents per pound. The evolution of prices over the post-war period is shown in Table 4–4.

The corporate income tax levied by the government of Peru was 35 per cent of profits. A depletion allowance of 15 per cent on direct cost was allowed but the proceeds were required to be reinvested in Peru. Fixed assets could be depreciated over a minimum of ten years or ten per cent of direct cost could be charged as depreciation, whichever was less. A.S. & R. requested a reduction of the corporate profits tax to 25 per cent, waiving of all import duties on its imported investment goods and exemption from the re-investment requirement for depletion. These concessions would be valid for the duration of the Exim-bank loan. Upon its complete amortization the tax regime would revert to the standard form and rates.

The labor force estimated to be employed at Toquepala numbered 4,000, during the construction period, and 3,500 during operation. Of these, about 250 were expected to be foreign personnel constituting about 75 per cent of the upper echelon management and technical personnel. The blue collar workers, numbering about 2,500 workers, would be drawn mainly from the highland agricultural region of Lake Titicaca, some 300 miles away, and were to be trained on the job.

The following information on factor prices is relevant.

a. *Labor:* The market wage equalled the opportunity and transfer cost.
b. *Capital:*

Bank interest on loans	13%
Interest on savings account	5%
Interest on mortgage bonds	9%
Rate of inflation	5%
Marginal productivity of capital (in real terms)	20%
Ratio of savings to GNP; upwards of	20%

c. *Foreign exchange:*
No exchange control.
Exchange rate in force since 1950:
Soles 15.00 = $1.00
Balance of payments is in equilibrium
Import duties average 20 per cent ad valorem.

To aid it in deciding whether or not to grant A.S. & R. the mining concession, the government was presented with two memoranda, one by A.S. & R. and another by a group that might have been called Committee for Defense of the National Patrimony. The former argues that the concession should be granted since Peru will benefit by:

a. Increased foreign exchange earnings;
b. Increased employment;
c. Stimulation of supplier industries; and
d. Training of work force.

The Committee, for its part, argues against the granting of the concession on the grounds that the investment will have been paid for in profits after nine years and the country will then be maintaining the foreign investors for another sixteen years at the expense of the exhaustion of Peru's natural resources.

For various reasons it is anticipated that Peru would only have the necessary managerial talent for running Toquepala five to ten years hence. Really competent managerial talent cannot be hired from the outside. The alternative to the A.S. & R. proposal therefore is to postpone the development of Toquepala for five to ten years. At that time a Peruvian company should be able to borrow from the Exim-Bank at conditions equal to those of A.S. & R., but would have to find the remaining $48 million of A.S. & R.

equity investment, locally. This is considered possible, albeit at the cost of sacrificing other investment projects.

Other things equal, the government would prefer a Peruvian company. It asks for the economic costs/benefits of opting for this alternative. Its negotiators need to know:

1. What price of copper shall Peru base its calculations on?

2. Does the A.S. & R. proposal contribute to Peru's growth? (If it does not benefit Peru, on balance, the following questions become unnecessary).

3. Would it be even better to postpone the exploitation of Toquepala until Peruvian entrepreneurs could undertake it?

4. What are the maximum concessions Peru can make to A.S. & R. while preserving a net benefit to the country, compared to the alternative of delaying the project?

5. What are the minimum concessions A.S. & R. needs to make the project attractive to it? (Consult Table 4–5 for the meager data available to the Government on the yield of U.S. private foreign investment in mining and smelting.)

Table 4–1 *Total Investment Cost*

Item	(*Millions of dollars*)
1. Acquisition and development to date	$ 8.00
2. Port of Ilo	3.90
3. Roads and truck equipment	4.90
4. Railroad	15.70
5. Water supply system	6.80
6. Towns	10.40
7. Shops for mine, mill, railroad	3.90
8. Power plant and transmission line	13.90
9. Mine: Preliminary stripping	32.40
Equipment	18.20
10. Concentrator	17.00
11. Smelter and smelter shops	19.00
12. Construction equipment	1.50
13. Working capital	12.50
Total Investment	$168.00

Table 4–2 *Expenditure of Funds*

	(*Millions of dollars*)
1. Assured purchases in the U.S. (at least)	$ 71.00
2. Spent, or to be spent, in Peru	42.00
3. Expenditure in U.S. or third countries	42.50
4. Working capital	12.50
Total	$168.00

Table 4–3   *Output and Operating Cost*

Item	First 10 Years	Next 15 Years
1. Annual production (tons of copper)	100,000	85,000
2. Unit costs in U.S. cents/lb. of copper:		
a. Mining, including waste stripping	4.190	4.870
b. Concentrating	1.870	2.807
c. Rail transport	0.267	0.287
d. Smelting	1.163	1.380
e. Ocean freight on blister	0.607	0.607
f. Refining in U.S.	1.530	1.530
g. General expenses	0.373	0.427
h. Contingencies	0.470	0.470
Total	10.470	12.380

Table 4–4   *Selected Copper Prices (U.S. Dollars/100 lbs.)*

	Prices				Unit Value of Exports	
Year	London	Antwerp (Congolese)	U.S. (Export)	Canada (Montreal)	Congo (Leopoldville)	Canada
1947	$23.48	—	$21.30	$18.83	—	—
1948	24.12	—	22.33	22.05	—	—
1949	22.99	—	19.44	20.37	—	—
1950	22.38	22.22	21.55	21.35	17.36	20.37
1951	27.58	27.40	26.26	26.28	23.14	27.52
1952	32.68	32.30	31.75	29.16	27.37	32.09

Table 4–5   *U.S. Foreign Investment In Mining and Smelting*

	1950			
	World	Canada	L. America	Other
Total assets	1689.6	567.8	789.7	118.6
U.S. investments, total	1128.5	334.3	628.4	56.5
Net earnings after foreign income tax[1]	191.0	79.9	74.8	12.8
U.S. share of net earnings[2]	147.9	52.1	68.5	9.6
Total U.S. income receipts[3]	111.9	31.0	64.4	2.9
U.S. share in undistributed profits of foreign corporations	32.6	17.7	4.1	6.5

Source: U.S. Department of Commerce, Office of Business Economics, *Foreign Investments of the United States, A supplement to the Survey of Current Business* (Washington: U.S. Government Printing Office, 1953), Appendix Table 28.

[1] Net profits of branches of U.S. corporations plus net profits applicable to common stock of foreign corporations.

[2] Net profit of branches of U.S. corporations, plus U.S. share in net earnings of foreign corporations applicable to common stockholders.

[3] Branch profits, preferred and common dividends, and interest.

Balance of Payments Decisions

Introduction

A government cannot escape the adoption of an explicit policy with respect to international economic relations—exports, imports, and invisible payments. An explicit policy is implied even if a country should adopt what is generally called a free trade policy, that is, one without any government-imposed barriers to relationships with the rest of the world. Most countries in fact prefer to influence or determine the foreign exchange rate and to influence the magnitude and composition of imports and exports by a mix of taxes and subsidies, usually in the form of import duties and export rebates or subsidies.

Government intervention in international economic transactions find their justification in part in long run development needs. Given a long time horizon the main considerations relate to the allocation of resources. In addition to the long run perspective, short run influences—resulting from frequent and widespread balance of payments crises—are of great importance in the formulation of international economic policy. Whatever their origin, their consequence is that the country pays out more foreign exchange than it earns in a given period. It runs down its reserves, incurs foreign debt, but eventually finds that it is unable to sustain these excessive out-payments over receipts for a continued period of time. The result is the need to undertake corrective measures.

The allocation rationale for foreign trade policy is usually stated explicitly or implicitly in terms of the principle of comparative advantage. In its simplest form, this principle affirms that a country ought to produce whatever it can produce best, regardless of the absolute level of its cost of production or efficiency. This simple maxim is difficult to translate into practice, however. The first problem that arises is whether comparative advantage should be interpreted to mean present or future comparative advantage—the old dichotomy between the static and the dynamic concepts. Obviously, today's production capabilities are important as a starting point. The conditions which will obtain in the domestic economy and in the world market one, two, three or five years from now are, however, also important. Therefore, it is necessay to strike a balance between conditions at different points in time in determining trade policy.

A further problem arises in ascertaining comparative advantage. One view is that a country has comparative advantage in whatever it in fact would export under worldwide free trade or under a policy of free trade adopted by the country alone. This view would lead to the policy perscription that in order to determine a country's comparative advantage, it should free its trade. The outcome of these policies is then presumed to be optimal since, by definition, it coincides with the country's comparative advantage. A different approach argues that comparative advantage is a concept subject to calculation *ex ante*. With suitable techniques, it is possible to determine in the absence of free trade what the country is best equipped to produce. If we accept the second view, the question then arises whether we want to determine what products a country is best equipped to produce or what processes it is best equipped to install. The alternative here is between considering the economy as vertically integrated and supplying its intermediate products from within the economy, or whether it specializes in a variety of subproducts and intermediate goods that are technologically separable.

Finally, if we consider economic policy at some point in time, we are not starting with a blank slate. Economic policy has existed in the past, and its consequences are reflected in the current economic structure of the country. Foreign trade policy designed under such circumstances must obviously take into account what has happened in the past: the investments in place, the skills acquired, the existing knowledge of materials and markets and so on.

The short run considerations involve the speed with which measures will be effective. To minimize the loss of reserves, speed in eliminating a balance of payments deficit is obviously desirable. Speed, however, is likely to have its costs. One cost may be a loss in the efficiency of allocation. Another may be the creation of unemployment and excess capacity. Thus, although speed is important to the solution of short run problems, its costs need to be weighed against the alternatives. For instance, it may be possible to obtain temporary balance of payments support from the IMF or elsewhere which will allow somewhat slower working but less costly policies to take hold and cure the situation.

The arsenal available to deal with balance of payments policy issues ranges from measures which affect relative prices and therefore change incentives to measures that are direct controls or quantitative restrictions. Various measures will have substantially different impacts on the balance of payments in the long term and the short term, as well as on the fiscal situation and income distribution. These two indirect effects can be important. It is of little use to prescribe, for example, a large export subsidy to boost exports, if the subsidies required can not be financed by the government. It is equally useless to prescribe a substantial increase in import duties if large scale smuggling is a possibility or if the possibilities of a tax payers' revolt makes these duties untenable. Finally, import or export duties or subsidies that have strong effects on the relative prices of food and other commodities may be self-negating by producing reactions in the wage rate or political reactions that make it unlikely that they can be maintained in the longer run.

A decision on the country's trade policy, then, must balance the requirements of growth, affected by the allocation of resources, against the requirements of effectiveness in the short term, and against fiscal and equity considerations essential to the feasibility of the policy package.

Suggested Readings on Balance of Payments Decisions (Cases 5, 6, 7)

The student is expected to be familiar with the starred (*) items.

Note that no exhaustive or detailed knowledge of the Colombian economy is required to solve these cases. Rather, emphasis will be placed on the interindustry techniques that can be used to solve these problems. For those interested in familiarizing themselves with the balance of payments problem specifically faced by Colombia, some suggested readings are listed at the end of the Country Background.

Interindustry Analysis

1. *Bruno, Michael. *Interdependence, Resource Use and Structural Change in Israel*. Jerusalem, Israel: Bank of Israel, 1962, chapters I, and IV sections 1–7.

2. Chenery, Hollis B., and Clark, Paul G. *Interindustry Economics*. New York: John Wiley and Sons, Inc., 1959, chapters I–IV.

Comparative Advantage and its Measurement

3. *Bruno, Michael. *Interdependence, Resource Use and Structural Change in Israel*. Jerusalem, Israel: Bank of Israel, 1962, chapter IV, section 8.

4. ————. "The Optimal Choice of Import-Substituting and Export-Promoting Projects." *Planning the External Sector: Techniques, Problems, and Policies*. New York: United Nations, 1967.

5. Balassa, Bela, and Schydlowsky, D. M. "Effective Tariffs, the Domestic Cost of Foreign Exchange and the Equilibrium Exchange Rate." *The Journal of Political Economy*, vol. 76, July 1968.

6. Vernon, Raymond. "International Investment and International Trade in the Product Cycle." *The Quarterly Journal of Economics*, vol. 80, May 1966, pp. 109–207.

7. Hirschman, Albert O. "The Political Economy of Import-Substituting Industrialization in Latin America." *The Quarterly Journal of Economics*, vol. 82, February 1968, pp. 1–32.

Import Restrictions

8. *Meade, J. E. *The Theory of International Trade: The Balance of Payments*. vol. 1. London: Oxford University Press, 1960, chps. XXI, "Types of Direct Control: Commercial Control," XXIII, "The Control of Imports and Exports," XXIV, "Direct Controls, Price Adjustment, and Economic Welfare."

9. ————. *Trade and Welfare.* London: Oxford University Press, 1955, chps. IX, "The Case for Free Trade," X, "Forms of Trade Control," section 1; XI, "Forms of Trade Control," section 2.

10. Haberler, G. *Quantitative Trade Controls: Their Causes and Nature.* Geneva: League of Nations, 1943.

11. Viner, J. *Trade Relations Between Free-Trade and Controlled Economies.* Geneva: League of Nations, 1943.

12. *Corden, W. M. "The Structure of a Tariff System and the Effective Protective Rate." *The Journal of Political Economy,* vol. 74, June 1966, pp. 221–237.

13. Guisinger, S. E. "Negative Value Added and the Theory of Effective Protection." *The Quarterly Journal of Economics,* vol. 83, August 1969, pp. 415–433.

Export Promotion

14. *Meade, J. E. *The Theory of International Trade: The Balance of Payments,* vol. 1. London: Oxford University Press, 1960, chapter XXIII, "The Control of Imports and Exports."

15. Urdinola, Antonio, and Mallon, R. D. "Policies to Promote Colombian Exports of Manufactures." (Economic Development Reports, #75) Cambridge: Development Advisory Service, Harvard University, 1967. Mimeographed.

16. Soligo, Ronald, and Stern, J. J. "Some Comments on the Export Bonus, Export Promotion and Investment Criteria." *Pakistan Development Review,* vol. 6, Spring 1966, pp. 38–56.

17. Schydlowsky, D. M. "Short Run Employment in Semi-Industrialized Economies." (Economic Development Reports, #73) Cambridge: Development Advisory Service, Harvard University 1967. Mimeographed. *Economic Development and Cultural Change* (early 1971).

Exchange Control

18. *Meade, J. E. *The Theory of International Trade:* The Balance of Payments, vol. 1. London: Oxford University Press, 1960, chps. XX, "Types of Direct Control: Financial Controls," and XXII, "The Control of Capital Movements."

19. Hirschman, Albert O. "Comments on Dr. Marshall's Paper." *Economic Development for Latin America.* Edited by Howard S. Ellis. (Proceedings of a conference held by the International Economic Association.) London: Macmillan and Co., Ltd., 1961, pp. 457–465.

Devaluation

20. *Meade, J. E. *The Theory of International Trade: The Balance of Payments,* vol. 1. London: Oxford University Press, 1960, chps. IX, "Financial Policy for Internal and External Balance," X, "Conflicts between Internal and External Balance," XI, "Price Adjustments as a Means of Policy."

21. *Machlup, F. "Relative Prices and Aggregate Spending in the Analysis of Devaluation." *The American Economic Review,* vol. 14, June 1955, pp. 255–278.

22. Orcutt, G. H. "Measurement of Price Elasticity in International Trade." *The Review of Economics and Statistics,* vol. 32, May 1950, pp. 117–132.

Interactions

23. Fleming, J. M. "Exchange Depreciation, Financial Policy and the Domestic Price Level." *International Monetary Fund Staff Papers,* vol. 6, April 1958, pp. 289–322.

24. Cohen, B. "Measuring the Short Run Impact of a Country's Import Restrictions on its Exports." *The Quarterly Journal of Economics,* vol. 80, August 1966, pp. 456–462.

25. Schydlowsky, D. M. "From Import Substitution to Export Promotion for Semi-Grown-Up Industries: A Policy Proposal." *The Journal of Development Studies,* vol. 3, July 1967, pp. 405–413.

Economic Integration

26. Lipsey, R. G. "The Theory of Custom Unions: A General Survey." *The Economic Journal,* vol. 70, September 1960, pp. 496–513.

27. Schydlowsky, D. M. "Analytical Basis for a National Policy of Regional Economic Integration in Latin America." *Journal of Common Market Studies,* vol. 6, December 1967, pp. 179–196.

28. Cooper, C. A., and Massel, B. F. "Toward a General Theory of Customs Unions for Developing Countries." *The Journal of Political Economy,* vol. 73, October 1965, pp. 461–476.

Country Background: Colombia

Colombia, with a territory of 440,000 square miles and a population of 18.7 million in mid-1967, had an average population density of only 43 persons/square mile. However, because of rivers and of the vast mountain ranges, the large majority of the population is concentrated in less than half the country's geographic area.

The mountainous and riverine terrain make transportation and communication difficult. At the same time the range in climatic conditions permits the growth of a wide variety of agricultural products ranging from wheat to tropical products, coffee and sugar. In some areas, agriculture is restricted by inadequate rainfall and low temperatures. While additional obstacles are imposed by the steep slopes of the Andes, in excess of 60 degrees at places, dense forest, poor drainage and soils in the lowlands, the agricultural potential of Colombia has not yet been fully exploited. Large forests have been virtually untouched by commercial lumbering and ocean fishing remains to be developed. The principal known mineral resources are petroleum deposits, which supply domestic consumption and around sixteen per cent of export earnings. Colombia is also the world's largest emerald producer. In addition, there exist coal and iron ore deposits in close proximity. At present these resources support a 170,000 ton steel mill, but they are estimated to be sufficient for a mill more than twice as large for the next forty years. Estimated coal deposits are 40 billion tons, perhaps the largest reserve in South America, but present production is only 2.5 million tons a year.

Economic Structure and Performance

Colombia's prime economic problem in recent years has been, and continues to be, the reconciliation of her aspirations for economic growth with a structural disequilibrium in the balance of payments. With a per capita GNP of approximately $300 in 1966, Colombia is not a very poor country, but its recent economic performance has not been satisfactory. A number of the specific economic difficulties encountered in the 1950s and early 1960s were related to the role of coffee in the economy. Although the share of agriculture in total GDP was less than 30 per cent in 1966, and coffee accounts for only about 25 per cent of that figure, it has been Colombia's major export commodity, accounting for almost 60 per cent of total export earnings in 1966. The fall in the coffee price from 71 cents per pound in 1954 to 37.8 cents per pound in 1963 was nothing short of a national disaster. Under the International Coffee Agreement the price has been stabilized in the range of 42 to 52 cents per pound, but the volume of Colombia's exports stagnated after the mid-1950s and the country's share of the world coffee market has declined by about one-third. In contrast with the $550

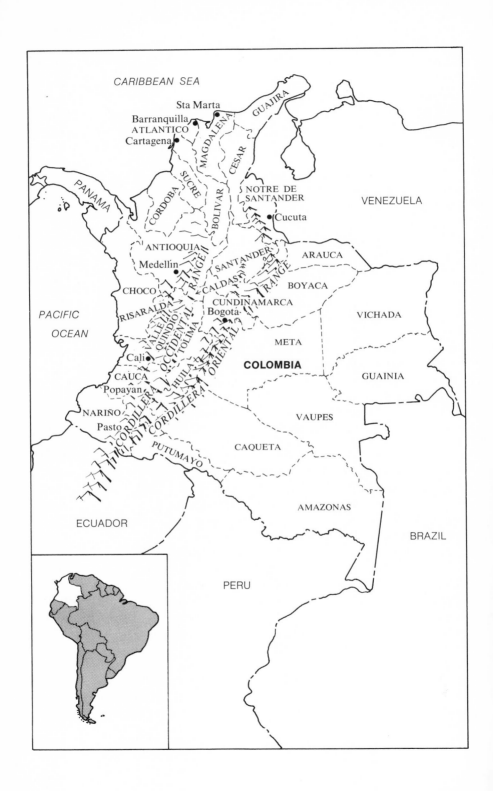

million of foreign exchange earned by coffee exports in 1954, receipts have fluctuated between $300 and $350 million in the 1960s and prospects are that they will not substantially exceed the latter figure until the mid-1970s.

In the years immediately following the coffee crisis, 1954–1958, real GDP grew only at a modest rate of 3.2 per cent per annum and on a per capita basis at less than one per cent. A major factor in the poor performance of the economy was the country's inability to import necessary raw materials and capital goods, following the collapse of the coffee market. During the period 1958–1962, the growth rate for real GDP increased to 5.3 per cent per annum, implying a 2.2 per cent per year increase in per capita GDP, but more recently the rate of growth has declined somewhat to a yearly rate of 4.4 per cent over the period 1962–1966.

In addition to its severe balance of payments problem, Colombia is faced with an extremely high rate of population growth. In the late 1940s the population growth rate was estimated at 2.6 per cent per annum. It soared to 3.2 per cent per annum in recent years and may be nearing 3.5 per cent at present. The few large metropolitan areas are growing at a rate in excess of seven per cent per year, and already have unemployment levels above ten per cent.

One of the basic objectives of the *Plan General* (1960–1970) is to diversify the economy and reduce its dependence on agriculture. Between 1950 and 1966, there was, in fact, a rapid growth of manufacturing. This was particularly rapid during 1950–1955, when Colombia was actively expanding its import substituting industries (such as steel, beverages, drugs). Subsequently the economy has continued to evolve in the same direction, but at a reduced rate.

Overall agricultural production increased at a yearly rate of 3.4 per cent during 1949/50 to 1964/65. More recently the growth rate has reached 4.0 per cent per annum, despite stagnation and even decline in coffee output. Foodgrain production has kept pace with population, although the pattern of production does not meet the dietary needs of the country.

Although agriculture contributed somewhat less than thirty per cent to GDP in 1966, it remains important in supplying exports and in providing employment. As in many less developed countries it suffers from low productivity and an excessive labor supply, leading to massive underemployment and very low per capita incomes. Although there are many modern commercial farms, the bulk of food is produced on small peasant-type farms using primitive methods, little farm equipment, fertilizer, or pesticides. Since modern tropical and subtropical agriculture is generally capital intensive, the process of commercialization and modernization of agriculture can lower food prices and increase the exportable surplus, but modernization is not likely to provide substantial employment opportunities.

Land reform could make some contribution to the dual problems of low productivity and underemployed agricultural labor. Colombia has both *latifundia* (estates, large farms) and *minifundia* (very small farms) and has had a long and varied history of land reform.[1] Although a land reform agency exists (El Institute Colombiano de la Reforma Agraria "IN-CORA"), 50,000 new farm families are formed yearly, making the task of colonization on underutilized *latifundia* immense. The long run solution to this problem may well lie in increasing employment elsewhere in the economy at a rate fast enough to absorb both the increase in population and the vast pool of landless *campesino* families.

Manufacturing is centered in three major cities—Bogotá, Cali and Medellin. Location is important because of the high domestic transportation costs resulting from the rugged terrain.

The manufacturing sector constituted less than 15 per cent of GDP in 1950 and nearly 20 per cent in 1967. The average rate of growth was 7.1 per cent for the period 1950–1956 and only 5.9 per cent for the period 1956–1966. Over half of the manufacturing sector's output consists of manufacturing industries producing nondurable consumer goods and textiles. The slow growth of per capita incomes, especially of the rural population, has played a major role in discouraging expansion of industrial activity.

Given the limited domestic market, some industries must export, if plants are to be operated at an efficient scale and at capacity. In 1965, industries which accounted for over 65 per cent of total value added operated at levels substantially below full capacity. Inadequate scale of plant and low rates of capacity utilization combine in Colombia with high rates of return on industrial investment made possible by tariffs and import controls. As a consequence both costs and prices are high, in turn preventing a rapid expansion of exports, which might otherwise supplement domestic demand and lower costs.

Colombia depends heavily on imports of capital and intermediate goods. However, since 1950 the rate of growth of capital goods production far exceeded that of the manufacturing sector as a whole. The average annual rate of growth of capital goods output during 1950–1962 was estimated at 17.5 per cent compared with 7.2 per cent for the whole manufacturing sector. By 1962, the ratio of domestically produced to imported capital goods had risen to nearly 20 per cent.

Inflationary expectations and fears of devaluation also had a retarding effect on industrial growth. During some periods restrictive monetary policy, an effort to control inflation, reduced the availability of working capital and, at various times, balance of payments problems led to shortages of imported raw materials and capital goods. The result of these and other factors were the modest growth rates of industrial output achieved in the last decade.

Recurrent inflationary pressures are indicated by the rising cost of living index. During the period 1950 to 1955 it increased at an annual rate of

---

[1] See Albert O. Hirschman, *Journeys Toward Progress* (New York: Twentieth Century Fund, 1963), chapter 2.

over seven per cent. From 1955 to 1962, the price level increased at a moderate rate of 3.1 per cent per annum but in 1962 the internal debt financing operations of the central government together with the sharp increases in wages and salaries authorized by the *Congreso Nacional* following the devaluation at the end of the year, put heavy pressure on prices. The crop failure of 1963 added to the pressure and as a result the cost of living index increased by 27.3 per cent in 1963 and by 17.7 per cent in 1964. Strict fiscal and monetary measures kept the price level fairly stable in 1965, but in 1966, the cost of living index again showed a rapid rise of over 16 per cent.

Savings and Investment

Investment, as a proportion of GDP, averaged over 20 per cent in 1954 to 1958. Following the collapse of the coffee market and the resultant stagnation of the economy, investment declined to 18 per cent and then to 16.0 per cent from 1962 to 1966. The marginal domestic savings rate, which reached 20.2 per cent from 1958 to 1962, has averaged only 15.0 per cent since then. Foreign savings financed approximately ten per cent of total gross capital formation since 1954. Public sector investment has averaged about 40 per cent of total investment in constant prices.

The major source of public sector savings is the central government. Tax revenues for the total public sector as a proportion of GDP have averaged only slightly more than ten per cent in the 1960s. As a consequence, Colombia ranks near the bottom of all Latin American countries with respect to taxes collected as a percentage of national income. Beginning in 1965 the Government made substantial efforts to increase revenues. While some attention was addressed to direct taxation the major effort was to increase indirect tax collections (sales tax). Nevertheless, taxes on foreign trade continue to be important and government revenues tend to fluctuate with the volume of imports. (Taxes on foreign trade constituted 26.9 per cent of total central government revenues in 1962 and rose to 37.5 per cent in 1966.) Taxes on property and income have declined, as a per cent of total revenues, from 57.5 per cent in 1962 to 39.1 per cent in 1966. Unlike most Latin American economies, the revenue system of Colombia has been characterized by a relatively high dependence on income and wealth taxes. This is changing, however, largely because past performance indicated that income taxes had an elasticity of less than one.

The failure to generate revenues adequate to finance government expenditure forced the national government to sell securities to the Banco de la Republica and to commercial banks. Sales to the central bank constitute primary credit expansion and contributed to the economy's inflationary pressure. Beginning in 1964, the Government acted to offset the inflationary dangers inherent in large scale credit expansion. Commercial bank reserve requirement rates were raised from 15 per cent to 24 per cent on demand deposits and from 10 to 17 per cent on time deposits.

The Foreign Sector

Colombia depends heavily on imported capital and intermediate goods, and a strong correlation exists between annual changes in investment and fluctuations in imports. Imported intermediate goods account for more than half of total input requirements in many industries. The relative importance of these import dependent industries is growing. In 1958, industries which imported more than 50 per cent of their inputs accounted for 37.9 per cent of total manufacturing value added; by 1962, such import dependent industries constituted 40.7 per cent of total value in manufacturing. Thus, the more dynamic industries—rubber, chemicals, metals, machinery—are relatively more import intensive than the industrial sector as a whole. Given the small margin of consumer goods imports, developments affecting Colombia's import capacity crucially affect the level of new investment and the utilization of installed capacity.

Imports must, of course, be financed by exports and net foreign capital inflows unless there is a drawing down of foreign exchange reserves. Unfortunately Colombia has for many years been heavily dependent upon exports of coffee and petroleum. During 1953 to 1955, coffee accounted for over 80 per cent of total export earnings, earning about U.S. $612 million per year or about $51 per capita. The average price was U.S. $0.6813 per pound. Prices declined steadily thereafter until by 1964 they reached U.S. $0.4880 per pound. In that year, coffee accounted for about 72 per cent of total exports and amounted to U.S. $548 million, or about U.S. $35 per capita. Thus, while total coffee export earnings declined by 10 per cent, on a per capita basis the decline was over 30 per cent.

Colombia's second major export commodity is petroleum, which has averaged between 10 and 15 per cent of total exports. While reserves are substantial, much of this oil is high cost. Unfortunately exports of crude oil have shown no significant upward trend since 1950, despite a steady increase in the volume of crude production. Domestic consumption has absorbed most of the increase in production, fostered by a low price for gasoline. In 1964, the price per gallon of gasoline in Bogotá was 1.36 pesos, equivalent to U.S. $0.106 per gallon, at the prevailing free market exchange rate. National and regional taxes added only about U.S. $0.012 per gallon. Except for Venezuela, Colombian gasoline prices and taxes on gasoline, are among the lowest in the world by a considerable margin.

As a result of the unfavorable price trend for coffee, and the failure to increase petroleum exports, Colombia's terms of trade and its capacity to import have declined steadily since 1954. Both the terms of trade index and the capacity to import index reached their nadir in 1963; the slight recovery in coffee since then has led to an improvement in both indices.

Like many developing countries, Colombia is highly dependent upon imports, but finances them largely from the sale of primary commodities for which international demand may be price and income inelastic. Deteriorating terms of trade since the mid-1950s, meant reduced imports. The result was to lower investment and utilization of capacity, leading to a reduction in domestic savings and a low rate of growth of per capita GDP. Only a very sharp curtailment of consumer goods imports and the rapid expansion of external official assistance after 1958 prevented a disastrous fall in investment. Even so, investment levels have fallen far short of plan targets and the levels required to make inroads on unemployment.

In response, Colombia has tried to stabilize coffee prices through the International Coffee agreement and to diversify the structure of exports. The trend in the volume of minor exports is encouraging. However, nearly all of these products continue to be related to Colombia's natural resource base (lumber, wood products, platinum) or to the agricultural sector (bananas, tobacco, cotton). The only major exceptions are textiles, cement and tires.

By 1960 Colombia applied three exchange rates to exports: A rate of 6.70 pesos per dollar for imports, Government transactions, and most freight charges; a free market rate that stood around 7.00 pesos per dollar for most private capital, tourism, and some miscellaneous items; and a rate of 6.40 pesos per dollar for coffee and petroleum. Inflation and continued balance of payments deficits forced the Government to devalue the peso in December 1962. The import rate was fixed at 9 pesos per dollar, the free market rate was pegged at 10 pesos per dollar, and the "coffee" rate was set at 7.10 pesos per dollar, moving up to 7.30 at the beginning of 1964. In October of that year, the Bank of the Republic ceased to support the free market, to discourage capital flight and encourage minor exports. By the middle of 1965, the free rate had reached almost 20 pesos per dollar in reaction to the impasse between the President and Congress over exchange and fiscal policy. The Bank of the Republic was suffering substantial losses by purchasing exchange from minor exporters at the free rate while selling it to importers at 9.00. It was therefore decided in June 1965 to establish an intermediate exchange market at 13.50 pesos per dollar, initially for minor exports and beginning in September for 75 per cent of imports. At this time the coffee rate was also moved up to 8.50 pesos per dollar. During the following twelve months import controls were progressively liberalized and goods still imported at the preferential rate of 9.00 were shifted to 13.50. Increased disbursements of foreign assistance were sufficient to keep external payments in balance until the last quarter of 1966, when a combination of adverse factors produced another exchange crisis.

Development Strategy

Colombia was one of the first countries in Latin America to complete a comprehensive economic and social development plan and to present it for review to the Committee of Nine under the provisions of the Charter of Punta del Este. The *Plan General de Desarollo* analyzed Colombia's economic structure and its development experience over the period 1950–1959 and, in light of available resources, set development targets for 1960–1970. The goals are to accelerate the rate of growth and to improve income distribution. This implies progressive industrialization and commercialization of the economy, with the industrial sector increasing its relative contribution to GDP and providing employment to a rising percentage of the labor force. The proximate objective of the *Plan General* was to achieve a rate of growth of GDP of 5.6 per cent per year over the period 1960–1964. Investment, as a proportion of GDP, was to rise to 25.3 per cent. The financing of the growth of fixed investment provided for in the *Plan General* was as follows: public savings 20.0 per cent; private savings 65.5 per cent; and net external resources 14.5 per cent. Virtually the entire responsibility for the investment program in manufacturing was left in the hands of the private sector.

The strategy for diversifying exports included adequate financial incentives, including in particular an adequate exchange rate, more effective institutional support for exporters; and domestic credit and investment policies to encourage increasing productivity in export manufactures.

Performance has so far fallen somewhat short of the targets with the balance of payments constraint appearing to be the main proximate culprit. A review of external sector policy is therefore of the greatest urgency.

Suggested Readings: Colombia

The student is expected to be familiar with starred (*) items.

1. Consejo Nacional de Politica Económica y Planeación, Departamento Administrativo de Planeación y Servicios Tecnicos. *Plan General de Desarrollo Económico y Social.* Cali: Editorial El Mundo, 1962.

2. *Sheehan, John. "Imports, Investment, and Growth—Colombia." *Development Policy—Theory and Practice.* Edited by G. F. Papanek. Cambridge: Harvard University Press, 1968, pp. 93–116.

3. ———, and Clark, Sara. "The Response of Colombian Exports to Variations in Effective Exchange Rates." Williams College, Center for Development Economics, Research Memorandum No. 11, June 1967. Mimeographed.

4. *Dunkerley, Harold B. "Exchange-Rate Systems in Conditions of Continuing Inflation-Lessons from Colombian Experience." *Development Policy—Theory and Practice.* Edited by G. F. Papanek. Cambridge: Harvard University Press, 1968, pp. 117–174.

5. Vanek, Jaroslav. *Estimating Foreign Resource Needs for Economic Development: Theory, Method, and a Case Study of Colombia.* (Economic Handbook Series) New York: McGraw-Hill Book Co., 1967, chapters III and IV.

6. United Nations, Economic Commission for Latin America (ECLA). *Analysis and Projections of Economic Development.* New York: Department of Economic and Social Affairs, United Nations, 1955, chapter III: "The Economic Development of Colombia."

7. Lovasy, G. "The International Coffee Market: A Note." *International Monetary Fund Staff Papers,* vol. 9, July 1962, pp. 226–242.

8. ———, and Bissonneault, L. "The International Coffee Market." *International Monetary Fund Staff Papers,* vol. II, November 1964, pp. 367–388.

9. International Bank for Reconstruction and Development (IBRD). *International Coffee Agreement, 1968.* Economics Departments, IBRD, Washington, D.C., August 1968. Mimeographed.

10. ———. *The Coffee Economy of Colombia.* Economics Department, IBRD (Working paper #15) Washington, D.C., 1968. Mimeographed.

11. Hirschman, Albert O. *Journeys Towards Progress.* New York: Twentieth Century Fund, 1963, chapter 2, "Land Use and Land Reform in Colombia."

Table Col.–1   *Gross Domestic Product of Colombia by Sector of Origin, 1950–1966*

	Gross Domestic Product	Agriculture	Manufacturing	All Others[1]
		(Millions of 1958 Pesos)		
1950	14,688.8	5,553.3	2,178.5	6,957.0
1951	15,146.6	5,622.4	2,246.8	7,277.4
1952	16,102.0	6,005.8	2,405.8	7,690.4
1953	17,081.0	6,017.7	2,642.6	8,420.7
1954	18,262.3	6,178.1	2,869.6	9,214.6
1955	18,976.1	6,327.2	3,062.8	9,586.1
1956	19,745.7	6,528.1	3,288.1	9,929.5
1957	20,186.2	6,928.1	3,437.8	9,820.3
1958	20,682.5	7,146.2	3,590.2	9,946.1
1959	22,128.6	7,504.8	3,888.8	10,735.0
1960	23,041.8	7,512.5	4,128.2	11,401.1
1961	24,179.0	7,807.6	4,375.8	11,995.6
1962	25,396.0	8,062.7	4,675.9	12,657.4
1963	26,238.0	8,106.0	4,898.6	13,233.4
1964	27,812.3	8,564.0	5,188.2	14,060.1
1965	28,701.7	8,559.6	5,431.5	14,710.6
1966	30,219.0	8,847.2	5,792.5	15,579.3

Source: Banco de la Republica.
[1] Includes: Fishing and hunting; mining; construction; commerce; transport; communications; electricity; gas; water; and Government.

Table Col.–2   *Expenditure on Gross Domestic Product: Colombia*

	Gross Domestic Product	Consumption	Gross Investment	Exports of Goods and Services	Imports of Goods and Services
		(Millions of pesos; Current prices)			
1950	7,860.5	6,477.9	1,324.7	853.3	795.4
1951	8,940.9	7,477.2	1,360.3	1,242.3	1,138.9
1952	9,650.9	8,063.8	1,492.6	1,286.5	1,192.0
1953	10,734.7	8,983.1	1,640.1	1,677.2	1,565.7

Table Col.–2 **(continued)**

	Gross Domestic Product	Consumption	Gross Investment	Exports of Goods and Services	Imports of Goods and Services
		(Millions of Pesos; Current prices)			
1954	12,758.8	10,567.8	2,142.0	1,907.5	1,858.5
1955	13,249.8	11,123.0	2,381.1	1,643.2	1,897.5
1956	14,862.8	12,191.7	2,704.6	1,846.0	1,879.5
1957	17,810.6	14,009.5	3,533.0	2,702.6	2,434.5
1958	20,682.5	16,201.0	3,862.6	3,889.9	3,271.0
1959	23,472.1	18,391.0	4,395.6	4,069.8	3,384.3
1960	26,417.6	20,937.7	5,476.6	4,163.9	4,160.6
1961	30,067.0	24,286.6	6,294.9	3,920.2	4,434.7
1962	33,578.4	27,446.2	6,393.4	4,146.4	4,407.8
1963	42,707.3	35,222.0	7,978.1	5,173.5	5,666.3
1964	52,699.3	43,757.8	9,734.8	6,376.5	7,169.4
1965	58,837.2	47,631.8	10,586.4	6,943.5	6,324.5
1966	72,020.7	59,426.8	14,867.8	8,435.9	10,709.8

Source: Banco de la Republica.

Table Col.–3   *Average Annual Growth Rates and Composition of GDP by Sectors of Origin,[1] 1950–1966 (Per cent)*

		Average Annual Growth Rates[2]					Composition	
		1950–56	1956–61	1961–66	1965	1966	1950	1966
1.	Gross Domestic Product	5.1	4.1	4.4	3.2	4.7	100.0	100.0
2.	Agriculture	2.7	3.6	2.7	−0.1	4.0	37.8	29.3
3.	Fishing & hunting	7.3	17.4	8.3	6.6	5.4	0.1	0.3
4.	Forestry	7.6	3.6	3.8	10.0	3.3	0.3	0.3
5.	Mining	5.1	3.6	4.9	7.4	−2.6	3.5	3.4
6.	Manufacturing	7.1	5.9	5.9	4.7	7.0	14.8	19.2
7.	Construction	10.8	1.7	−0.6	−5.8	−1.0	2.7	3.0
8.	Commerce	5.1	3.8	4.8	4.2	5.0	15.7	16.0
9.	Transport	9.2	2.7	4.3	2.8	5.9	5.0	5.9
10.	Communications	9.9	8.4	10.8	11.2	7.2	0.4	0.8
11.	Electricity, gas, water	10.0	9.3	9.0	9.2	2.8	0.5	1.0
12.	Government	5.5	4.3	5.5	5.5	3.9	4.6	5.0
13.	Other	5.2	6.8	3.5	5.9	6.0	14.6	15.8

Source: Banco de la Republica.
[1] Based on data in constant 1958 prices.
[2] With respect to previous year or over indicated time period.

Table Col.–4 *Composition of Expenditure on GDP, 1950–1966 (Per cent)*

	Gross Domestic Product	Consumption	Gross Investment	Exports of Goods and Services	Imports of Goods and Services
1950	100.0	82	17	11	10
1955	100.0	84	18	12	14
1960	100.0	79	21	16	16
1965	100.0	81	18	12	11
1966	100.0	83	20	12	15

Source: Calculated from data of Table 2.

Table Col.–5 *Investment and its Financing, 1950–1966*

		1950–51	1952–54	Average Values for Period 1954–58 (Per cent)	1958–62	1962–66
1.	Total Investment/ GDP	16.0	15.9	18.4	19.7	18.3
2.	Foreign Savings/GDP	—	0.1	1.9	1.8	2.1
3.	National Savings/ GDP	16.1	15.9	16.7	18.1	16.4
4.	Resource Gap/GDP	−1.0	−0.8	0.8	0.4	0.6
5.	Domestic Savings/ GDP	17.0	16.6	17.6	19.3	17.7
6.	Marginal Savings Rate	—	15.2	18.6	20.2	15.0
7.	Foreign Savings/[1] Total Investment	0.1	0.9	10.3	9.2	11.5
8.	National Savings/ Total Investment	99.9	99.1	89.7	90.8	88.5
9.	Resource Gap/[2] Total Investment	−6.3	−4.8	4.4	2.0	3.1
10.	Domestic Savings/ Total Investment	106.3	104.8	95.6	98.0	96.9

Source: Banco de la Republica.
[1] Balance of payments deficit on current account, excluding transfers.
[2] Balance of payments deficit on current account excluding transfers and factors.

Table Col.–6   *Cost of Living Index for Workers (Percentage increase over previous period)*

	Total Index	Foodstuffs
1958	13.2	12.3
1959	8.2	7.5
1960	5.7	4.9
1961	8.5	10.6
1962	4.3	1.1
1963	27.3	32.1
1964	17.7	24.2
1965	7.0	4.3
1966	16.7	18.2

Source: Dirección Administrativa Nacional de Estadistica.

Table Col.–7   *Colombia: Balance of Trade (Millions of dollars)*

Year	Exports (FOB)	Imports (CIF)	Balance
1950	407.8	363.0	+44.8
1951	474.1	415.9	+58.2
1952	486.9	415.4	+71.5
1953	621.9	546.7	+75.2
1954	670.2	671.8	−1.6
1955	588.0	669.3	−81.3
1956	606.9	657.2	−50.3
1957	522.3	482.6	+39.7
1958	472.7	399.9	+72.8
1959	458.9	415.6	+43.3
1960	440.5	518.6	−78.1
1961	441.5	557.1	−115.6
1962	440.5	540.4	−99.9
1963	460.4	506.0	−45.6
1964	601.0	586.3	+14.7
1965	551.0	453.5	+97.5
1966^p	492.2	672.1	−179.9
Average:			
1950–1956	550.8	534.2	(+16.6)
1960–1966	488.1	513.2	(−25.1)

Source: Banco de la Republica as reported in *I.M.F. Balance of Payments Yearbook.*
^{p} Provisional

Table Col.–8 Composition of Colombian Imports (CIF), 1950–1966 (Millions of dollars)

Year	Consumer Goods	Fuels	Construction Materials	Raw and Intermediate Goods	Capital Goods	Unclassified	Total
1950	76.0	10.2	25.0	129.7	120.3	1.8	363.0
1951	74.1	16.6	26.9	160.1	136.0	2.2	415.9
1952	74.3	19.3	27.8	141.3	150.4	2.2	415.4
1953	104.9	25.6	43.9	158.8	210.3	3.2	546.7
1954	144.1	29.8	52.5	193.9	246.9	4.5	671.8
1955	114.8	24.7	51.9	210.2	263.4	4.3	669.3
1956	80.6	23.2	56.6	229.6	263.3	3.9	657.2
1957	53.3	19.1	40.0	213.5	152.0	4.7	482.6
1958	32.8	9.8	32.9	191.4	128.8	4.2	399.9
1959	30.3	8.6	20.4	204.2	149.3	2.8	415.6
1960	34.6	10.3	23.6	229.7	216.4	4.0	518.6
1961	48.1	12.5	24.7	238.2	228.3	5.3	557.1
1962	36.0	13.5	25.7	243.9	208.1	12.8	540.0
1963	31.4	9.3	24.2	234.0	195.7	11.4	506.0
1964	37.1	6.4	27.3	268.0	236.5	11.0	586.3
1965	23.6	54.9[a]		210.0	165.0	[a]	453.5
1966	61.2			381.1[b]		17.4	672.1

Source: 1950–1964: John Sheahan "Imports, Investment and Growth—Colombia." Reprinted by permission of the publishers from Gustav F. Papanek, ed. *Development Policy: Theory and Practice* Cambridge, Mass.: Harvard University Press, Copyright, 1968, by the President and Fellows of Harvard College, p. 95.
[a] Includes unclassified imports.
[b] Includes fuels and constuction material.
Note: "Many arbitrary decisions enter any such classification, and it has not been possible to check the consistency of all those which underlie this one. In particular, the figures for 1950–57 are quite doubtful. This statement is based on the results of a thorough recheck of previously published data made by the Department of Planning for the years from 1958 onward. The data from 1958 are thus on a more solid basis, but even for this period it is necessary to bear in mind that contraband imports are not registered anywhere." (Sheahan, p. 95).

Table Col.-9 *Composition of Colombian Exports (FOB), 1950–1966 (Millions of dollars)*

	1950	1952	1954	1956	1958	1960	1962	1964	1966ᵖ
Registered Exports									
1. Coffee	303.1	370.1	549.3	469.6	354.5	304.2	305.6	423.0	312.8
2. Bananas	15.0	16.9	20.2	27.8	15.5	12.5	9.8	13.3	19.1
3. Tobacco	2.1	1.6	2.3	3.0	1.9	2.2	6.2	10.1	5.3
4. Cotton	—	—	—	—	—	11.5	14.4	6.7	2.1
5. Wood	0.1	0.2	2.0	1.6	1.3	1.9	2.0	4.2	2.8
6. Platinum	1.3	1.8	1.8	2.1	1.0	1.1	0.9	1.6	—
7. Cement	0.6	0.3	0.3	1.1	1.2	1.8	1.8	2.5	2.0
8. Fuel oil	—	—	—	2.7	10.1	6.9	6.5	7.8	9.2
9. Petroleum	64.2	73.2	70.7	69.2	66.6	73.2	55.8	80.5	67.3
10. Refined sugar	2.2	0.5	—	4.3	—	—	6.8	3.5	7.9
11. Non-monetary gold	12.3	13.7	13.2	14.7	12.0	15.1	13.9	12.8	9.6
12. Others	6.9	8.6	10.4	10.8	8.6	10.1	17.8	35.0	54.1
Total A:	407.8	486.9	670.2	606.9	472.7	440.5	440.5	601.0	492.2
Contraband Exports									
1. Coffee	—	—	—	61.5	11.4	10.0	10.0	10.0	10.0
2. Cattle	—	—	—	—	14.4	14.4	8.5	12.0	10.0
3. Textiles	—	—	—	—	40.6	30.6	16.5	13.0	10.0
4. Others	—	—	—	—	—	—	—	—	15.0
Total B:	—	—	—	61.5	66.4	55.0	35.0	35.0	45.0
Total A + B	407.8	486.9	670.2	668.4	539.1	495.5	475.5	636.0	537.2

Source: Totals from *I.M.F. Balance of Payments Yearbooks*. Commodity breakdown as shown in: IBRD, *Current Economic Position and Prospects of Colombia*, vol. 1 (May 23, 1967).
ᵖ Provisional

Table Col.–10 *Colombia Balance of Payments, 1950–1966 (Millions of dollars)*

Item	1950 Cr	1950 Dt	1953 Cr	1953 Dt	1956 Cr	1956 Dt	1959 Cr	1959 Dt
A. *Goods and Services*	432.2	444.9	665.7	649.8	733.3	747.2	610.4	550.1
1. Merchandise (FOB)	407.8	336.2	621.9	523.8	668.4	598.8	527.9	402.5
2. Freight and insurance on merchandise	7.0	8.5	12.3	20.0	16.5	19.3	24.5	17.6
3. Other transportation	1.5	13.5	3.6	21.9	10.0	36.0	9.6	35.8
4. Travel	6.8	13.4	10.9	20.2	9.0	21.6	17.3	22.5
5. Investment income	—	39.3	—	22.8	—	16.0	1.4	37.7
a. Direct investment	—	(35.7)	—	(11.0)	—	(10.8)	—	(18.7)
b. Other	—	(3.6)	—	(11.8)	—	(5.2)	(1.4)	(19.1)
6. Other services, nei	9.1	34.0	17.0	41.1	29.4	55.5	29.7	33.9
Net goods and services	—	12.7	15.9	—	—	139.0	60.3	—
B. *Transfer Payments*	—	0.8	1.1	1.9	3.5	2.0	4.1	1.7
1. Private	—	0.8	—	1.9	2.2	2.0	1.7	1.2
2. Official	—	—	1.1	—	1.3	—	2.4	0.5
Net Transfer Payments	—	0.8	—	0.8	1.5	—	2.4	—
C. *Capital and Monetary Gold*	75.0	44.2	81.2	78.2	183.0	97.8	155.2	191.7
I. *Non-monetary sectors*	—	—	—	—	—	—	81.3	29.2
1. Direct investment	—	—	—	—	—	—	0.9	—
2. Other private long term	—	—	—	—	—	—	41.5	8.1
3. Other private short term	—	—	—	—	—	—	26.4	—
4. Local and central government	—	—	—	—	—	—	12.5	21.1
II. *Monetary sectors*	—	—	—	—	—	—	73.9	162.5
1. Private institutions	—	—	—	—	—	—	4.5	2.4
2. Central bank	—	—	—	—	—	—	69.4	160.1
3. Monetary gold	—	(22.3)	—	(10.1)	(28.4)	—	(0.8)	—
D. *Net Errors and Omissions*	—	17.3	—	18.1	—	72.8	—	26.2

Table Col.–10 (continued)

Item	1960 Cr	1960 Dt	1961 Cr	1961 Dt	1962 Cr	1962 Dt	1963 Cr	1963 Dt
A. Goods and Services	591.5	676.4	578.1	720.7	571.4	747.0	590.2	736.1
1. Merchandise (FOB)	495.3	496.4	476.5	530.8	475.8	536.9	485.4	497.5
2. Freight and insurance on merchandise	27.8	20.9	29.6	23.6	33.4	29.7	32.7	26.4
3. Other transportation	11.3	48.8	13.2	49.4	14.7	49.8	16.2	34.4
4. Travel	22.7	28.3	22.6	24.1	12.6	22.8	19.3	25.0
5. Investment income	2.4	42.0	0.4	50.8	—	57.3	—	80.6
a. Direct investment	—	(27.1)	—	(36.0)	—	(34.7)	—	(39.4)
b. Other	(2.4)	(14.9)	(0.4)	(14.8)	—	(22.6)	—	(41.2)
6. Other services, nei	32.0	40.0	35.8	42.0	34.9	50.5	36.6	72.2
Net goods and services	—	84.9	—	142.6	—	175.6	—	145.9
B. Transfer Payments	8.4	2.7	11.4	2.8	17.4	3.5	22.7	4.4
1. Private	2.6	2.2	3.1	2.3	7.5	2.3	11.8	3.0
2. Official	5.8	0.5	8.3	0.5	9.9	1.2	10.9	1.4
Net Transfer Payments	5.7	—	8.6	—	13.9	—	18.3	—
C. Capital and Monetary Gold	227.2	123.4	273.5	130.2	373.4	244.8	440.5	238.7
I. Non-monetary sectors	136.9	42.2	139.8	74.9	140.3	57.3	250.7	81.9
1. Direct investment	2.5	—	6.2	—	10.4	—	17.8	—
2. Other private long term	54.2	5.5	41.0	47.6	49.4	12.6	125.5	12.0
3. Other private short term	68.6	11.7	31.0	—	18.5	22.6	32.5	45.5
4. Local and central government	11.6	25.0	61.6	27.3	62.0	22.1	74.9	24.4
II. Monetary sectors	90.3	81.2	133.7	55.3	233.1	187.5	189.8	156.8
1. Private institutions	11.4	2.4	2.6	9.0	8.4	7.2	5.5	1.4
2. Central bank	78.9	78.8	131.1	46.3	224.7	180.3	184.3	155.4
3. Monetary gold	—	(7.2)	—	(10.2)	(30.8)	—	—	(4.3)
D. Net Errors and Omissions	—	24.6	—	9.3	33.1	—	—	74.2

Table Col.–10 (continued)

Item	1964 Cr	1964 Dt	1965 Cr	1965 Dt	1966ᵖ Cr	1966ᵖ Dt
A. *Goods and Services*	748.6	885.2	708.5	725.6	682.9	965.5
1. Merchandise (FOB)	636.0	575.4	591.0	423.5	537.2	627.6
2. Freight and insurance on merchandise	36.5	36.0	43.5	28.9	42.2	37.3
3. Other transportation	19.4	60.0	18.3	60.4	17.8	77.7
4. Travel	24.6	54.9	27.5	50.2	28.2	54.4
5. Investment income	—	73.2	—	79.2	—	92.3
a. Direct investment	—	(16.1)	—	(24.9)	—	(28.4)
b. Other	—	(57.1)	—	(54.3)	—	(63.9)
6. Other services, nei	32.1	85.7	28.2	83.4	57.5	76.2
Net goods and services	—	136.6	—	17.1	—	282.6
B. *Transfer Payments*	18.7	4.3	15.9	4.0	6.5	2.4
1. Private	8.2	3.0	7.2	3.0	5.2	—
2. Official	10.5	1.3	8.7	1.0	1.3	2.4
Net Transfer Payments	14.4	—	11.9	—	4.1	—
C. *Capital and Monetary Gold*	466.9	188.2	221.3	270.4	313.9	104.2
I. *Non-monetary sectors*	363.7	100.6	145.8	146.0	227.7	77.2
1. Direct investment	66.1	—	22.4	—	—	4.9
2. Other private long term	106.9	21.1	61.9	16.4	—	9.4
3. Other private short term	114.7	45.3	—	103.2	112.1	—
4. Local and central government	76.0	34.2	61.5	26.4	115.6	62.9
II. *Monetary sectors*	103.2	87.6	75.5	124.4	86.2	27.0
1. Private institutions	5.9	7.8	18.6	1.2	7.0	—
2. Central bank	97.3	79.8	56.9	123.2	79.2	27.0
3. Monetary gold	(3.6)	—	(23.1)	—	(9.0)	—
D. *Net Errors and Omissions*	—	156.5	54.3	—	68.8	—

ᵖ Provisional

Table Col.–11 *Interindustry Table of Colombia, 1954*

Sector No.	*Sectoral Definitions*
1.	Agriculture, forestry, fishing
2.	Mining and quarrying
3.	Handicrafts, cottage industry
4.	Food processing
5.	Alcoholic and non-alcoholic beverages
6.	Cigarettes and tobacco products
7.	Textiles, clothing, and finished textiles
8.	Wood and cork
9.	Furniture
10.	Paper and paper products
11.	Printing of books and newspapers
12.	Tanning of leather and manufacture of leather products
13.	Rubber and rubber products
14.	Chemicals
15.	Coal and petroleum products
16.	Non-metallic minerals
17.	Basic metals
18.	Metal products
19.	Non-electrical machinery
20.	Electrical machinery
21.	Transport equipment
22.	Miscellaneous industries
23.	Construction
24.	Services
25.	Total interindustry flows
31.	Imports (cif)
32.	Gross value added
33.	Gross value of product
41.	Exports
42.	Government consumption
43.	Private consumption
44.	Investment (gross; fixed)
45.	Changes in stocks
46.	Total final demand
47.	Total value of output

Table Col.–11 (continued)   Colombia Domestic Flow Matrix, 1954 (1000's of pesos)

	1 Agric	2 Mines	3 Hndct	4 Foods	5 Bvrgs	6 Tobac	7 Txtls	8 Wood	9 Furnt	10 Paper	11 Print
1 Agric	231330	37	74307	2564000	7000	29602	57728	13471	108	103	6
2 Mines	2172	145	10719	16665	118	2	393	20	4	20	1
3 Hndct	21151	6674	29356	565	405	20	2753	4926	2225	–0	–0
4 Foods	30973	–0	43461	193920	36220	22	1304	26	–0	102	2
5 Bvrgs	–0	–0	2088	–0	26575	1	–0	17	123	23	5
6 Tobac	–0	–0	1453	–0	–0	4578	–0	–0	–0	–0	–0
7 Txtls	629	724	197450	10394	215	3	311570	105	1789	275	1241
8 Wood	1164	3269	–0	346	364	23	760	6878	3441	8	37
9 Furnt	4203	241	240	116	–0	–0	–0	93	257	–0	–0
10 Paper	–0	492	2770	9068	480	961	1586	42	39	9307	1483
11 Print	–0	109	1378	691	1869	1789	171	49	–0	3	11
12 Lther	–0	22	34009	7	–0	–0	1272	7	260	2	5
13 Rubbr	–0	–0	2708	332	196	–0	135	3	45	2	23
14 Chems	5489	1279	40505	1863	4900	11	34085	271	1607	1107	315
15 Petro	16779	4130	4563	4632	2706	81	135	3	1	89	–0
16 Nmm	9237	468	14141	615	6789	–0	841	66	216	11	108
17 Metal	62	–0	6790	121	–0	–0	79	39	188	–0	39
18 Mtlpd	63	3204	13137	2592	11784	–0	834	402	441	5	1
19 Nemac	206	–0	–0	2886	–0	61	2162	–0	5	112	116
20 Elmac	–0	–0	4220	–0	–0	–0	–0	11	–0	–0	–0
21 Tnpeq	–0	–0	13176	52	103	1058	–0	–0	–0	–0	–0
22 Other	288	–0	10228	2343	–0	–0	1102	–0	9	1111	206
23 Const	–0	–0	–0	–0	–0	–0	–0	–0	–0	–0	–0
24 Srvcs	114000	46409	74531	371910	100720	14102	129410	12722	6314	16653	30110
25 Sum	437690	67203	581230	3183100	200450	52314	546320	39151	17081	28933	33709
31 Imprt	48663	16597	16570	98453	21143	4044	77215	1183	1658	15215	24067
32 Gva	5097208	319100	500000	281866	356744	200195	442084	19383	19766	23780	62471
33 Tgo	5583561	402900	1097802	3563389	578336	256553	1065616	59717	38505	67928	120247

Table Col.–11 (continued)

	12 Lther	13 Rubbr	14 Chems	15 Petro	16 Nmm	17 Metal	18 Mtlpd	19 Nemac	20 Elmac	21 Tnpeq	22 Other
1 Agric	932	1279	3570	413	93	2103	16	13	5	32	16
2 Mines	625	41	3117	96379	21627	9806	15	2	3	-0	258
3 Hndct	-0	-0	4360	-0	9808	2590	5131	1488	1239	4665	2069
4 Foods	26359	-0	9405	-0	30	-0	7	-0	2	-0	5
5 Bvrgs	-0	-0	775	-0	5	-0	1	-0	6	-0	1
6 Tobac	-0	-0	-0	-0	-0	-0	-0	-0	-0	-0	-0
7 Txtls	1790	3242	1296	-0	38	1	675	-0	50	169	262
8 Wood	651	29	1927	-0	432	2	570	47	44	129	18
9 Furnt	-0	-0	-0	-0	-0	-0	-0	-0	301	-0	-0
10 Paper	1009	135	4794	-0	7830	3	669	249	283	1	446
11 Print	-0	-0	546	-0	24	-0	9	-0	-0	-0	44
12 Lther	32786	271	26	-0	-0	6	72	27	5	27	21
13 Rubbr	1028	8604	19	-0	1	525	66	-0	712	291	49
14 Chems	6136	248	19168	82	3493	3555	1155	84	-0	953	188
15 Petro	48	10	679	2098	124	794	317	101	184	26	109
16 Nmm	31	4	2936	29	18602	47	47	2	1079	16	16
17 Metal	4	2	377	320	733	138550	10101	2021	68	267	4249
18 Mtlpd	396	3	943	-0	485	168	793	117	-0	107	21
19 Nemac	71	150	239	-0	1602	-0	48	172	701	3	36
20 Elmac	-0	-0	-0	-0	-0	3	7	15	1	52	-0
21 Tnpeq	-0	-0	-0	-0	-0	-0	8	2	-0	1941	-0
22 Other	6	23	720	-0	57	1	7	36	-0	6	283
23 Const	-0	-0	-0	-0	-0	-0	-0	-0	-0	-0	-0
24 Srvcs	22457	23860	60078	17950	26760	20533	25693	5198	9612	12062	8140
25 Sum	94329	37901	114970	117270	91744	178640	45470	9574	14295	20756	16231
31 Imprt	10188	24036	36661	815	16689	6668	25637	5708	16037	14624	7808
32 Gva	59605	52850	129076	52765	131810	38987	47951	14907	22467	41276	27902
33 Tgo	164122	114787	280712	170851	240243	224296	119058	30189	52799	76656	51941

Table Col.–11 (continued)

	23 Const	24 Srvcs	25 Sum	41 Xprts	42 Gcons	43 Pcons	44 Invst	45 Sticks	46 Fnldm	47 Output
1 Agric	163250	6656	3156000	72513	-0	2328416	42100	-15500	2427529	5583561
2 Mines	33967	11011	207109	172219	-0	23208	-0	363	195790	420900
3 Hndct	24103	127380	250911	-0	9187	837708	-0	-0	846895	1097802
4 Foods	-0	2740	344570	1464908	-0	1737045	-0	16861	3218814	3563389
5 Bvrgs	-0	807	30427	3	-0	538895	-0	9011	547909	578336
6 Tobac	-0	-0	6031	51	-0	243947	-0	6524	250522	256553
7 Txtls	-0	39185	571100	1257	-0	478040	-0	15216	494513	1065616
8 Wood	26414	6667	53220	1754	1797	1557	447	942	6497	59717
9 Furnt	3234	1488	10173	152	1303	18446	6769	1662	28332	38505
10 Paper	1701	15994	59351	3	8098	236	-0	240	8577	67928
11 Print	84	66003	72780	22	24689	18023	-0	4733	47467	120247
12 Lther	-0	4303	73117	3095	-0	81935	383	5592	91005	164122
13 Rubbr	5601	68652	87766	76	1881	9931	-0	15133	27021	114787
14 Chems	8298	31456	163930	1370	27594	82148	-0	5670	116782	280712
15 Petro	11409	72344	123950	4380	11284	21409	-0	9830	46903	170851
16 Nmm	10567	26219	187040	2498	379	5941	-0	44387	53205	240243
17 Metal	25209	3288	193520	645	-0	-0	6577	23555	30777	224296
18 Mtlpd	10771	21766	68101	742	403	20731	20243	8838	50957	119058
19 Nemac	-0	2048	9917	1587	-0	3355	15198	132	20272	30189
20 Elmac	-0	-0	5009	82	-0	38163	7727	1818	47790	52799
21 Tnpeq	17	34495	50853	24	4252	15542	6386	-401	25803	76656
22 Other	-0	2018	18447	267	1314	28736	129	3048	33494	51941
23 Const	-0	-0	-0	-0	-0	-0	1544046	-0	1544046	1544046
24 Srvcs	227350	587280	1963900	195531	149609	4142392	240786	-0	4728318	6692175
25 Sum	647080	1131800	7707200	-0	-0	-0	-0	-0	-0	-0
31 Imprt	146856	145377	-0	-0	-0	-0	-0	-0	-0	-0
32 Gva	750113	5415000	-0	-0	-0	-0	-0	-0	-0	-0
33 Tgo	1544046	6692175	-0	-0	-0	-0	-0	-0	-0	-0

Table Col.–12   *Wage Component of Value Added (Millions of pesos)*

Sector	Wages	Wages as a Per Cent of Value Added
1. Agriculture	3027.7	59%
2. Mining	258.3	81
3. Handicrafts, etc.	—	—
4. Food processing	232.7	83
5. Alcoholic and non-alcoholic beverages	67.7	19
6. Cigarettes and tobacco products	45.6	23
7. Textiles, etc.	158.1	36
8. Wood and cork	6.6	34
9. Furniture	7.7	39
10. Paper and paper products	7.5	31
11. Printing of books, etc.	31.7	51
12. Tanning and bather manufactures	22.4	38
13. Rubber and rubber products	12.0	23
14. Chemicals	36.7	28
15. Coal and petroleum products	28.5	54
16. Non-metallic minerals	40.9	31
17. Basic metals	16.3	42
18. Metal products	20.0	42
19. Non-electrical machinery	6.2	42
20. Electrical machinery	9.4	42
21. Transport equipment	17.2	42
22. Miscellaneous industries	10.4	37
23. Construction	—	—
24. Services	—	—

Note: Data for sectors 17–21 assumes ratio of wages to value added equal for all machinery producing sectors.

Table Col.–13   *Foreign Exchange Reserves*

Year	Millions of US Dollars
1950	113
1953	202
1956	131
1959	215
1962	85
1965	96
1966	77

Source: International Monetary Fund, *International Financial Statistics* Supplement to 1967/68 Issues; September 1969.

Case 5: Export Promotion Policy

Colombia's export earnings have shown a generally declining trend since 1956. At the same time imports have continued their upward trend. The result has been a deterioration of the balance of trade. Prior to 1956 the economy was marked by a high growth rate made possible by Colombia's ability to finance rapidly rising imports, particularly of investment goods. A continuation of the rapid rate of growth would have required a further rise in export earnings. The failure to increase earnings from exports is thus a major factor in the economy's inability to maintain its earlier buoyancy.

The decline in Colombia's export earnings[1] was primarily due to the fall in the international price of coffee. The price of this crucial export promises to be more stable under the International Coffee Agreement but by the end of 1966 the government is convinced that a coffee boom cannot be relied upon to generate an upturn in the country's export revenue and growth rate. As a result, the government is interested in formulating and implementing a broadly based export promotion policy that will allow the economy to recapture its earlier growth rate.

Among the more important considerations which must be taken into account in formulating an export promotion policy are the following:

1. Almost all manufactured exports require some inputs of imported goods either in the form of raw materials or intermediate goods. The latter may be directly imported or may be imported raw materials processed into domestic goods that are themselves inputs into the manufacture of export goods. Thus a dollar's worth of exports does not necessarily increase foreign exchange availability by one dollar.

2. Whereas Colombia can sell almost any of its minor exports at a constant price, the same is not true for Colombia's major export commodity, coffee. Here the marginal revenue is less than the price of coffee, thus making it less desirable to expand coffee exports.

3. Colombia has access to the markets of the Latin American Free Trade Area (LAFTA) under preferential conditions. It is therefore able to place a limited quantity of merchandise, except coffee, in this market at prices above world market levels. This preference is not uniform for all commodities and it thus makes some commodities particularly good foreign exchange earners. No information on the size of these preferences, or the size of market they imply, is readily available.

4. The past pattern of import substitution in Colombia has been such that, given the need to hold down imports to reduced foreign exchange receipts (which is being achieved through import restrictions and deflationary aggregate policies), there is substantial excess capacity in most manufacturing sectors. At the same time there is also considerable industrial unemployment. Whereas this implies a zero shadow price of labor and capital in the short run, up to full capacity utilization, the employment

[1] See Tables Col.-7 and Col.-10 for the relevant information on Colombia's foreign sector.

effects will vary across sectors and the increased exports in different sectors will have different employment effects.

Some of these problems are best handled in an interindustry framework. An input-output table for 1954, prepared by the Colombian Planning Commission, is reproduced in Table Col.–11. (While admittedly a table referring to the year 1954 is somewhat dated for an analysis of conditions in 1966, no more recent table is available.) Transactions are valued at market prices except for imports which are shown at their CIF price. The relationship between market and CIF prices is given in Table 5–1.

A further question is the principal policy instrument to be used in increasing exports. The main alternatives are devaluation and subsidization. Whether these measures will be applied on a nondiscriminatory basis between products or whether they will be applied to different products in a different manner or magnitude must also be decided.

The Colombian Planning Commission asks that the following issues be considered:

1. Given excess capacity in all manufacturing sectors, in which sectors or commodities should exports be expanded in the short run? What are the likely employment effects of this policy?

2. Past experience has shown that full capacity operation is reached following two to three years of rapid expansion.[2] When, as a result of the export promotion policy, this point is reached, should the government's policy be modified to favor different commodities from those first chosen? If so, which commodities should be favored? Should this alternative list of goods have been chosen initially?

3. Given a substantial stock of surplus coffee[3] and the International Coffee Agreement, what should Colombia's policy be with respect to this crop? Is continued participation in the Coffee Agreement in Colombia's interest? This is one issue where adequate information may not be available. If so, the Commission would like to know what information it needs to decide on coffee policy and how it can go about obtaining this information. Any policy prescription has to take account of the possibility, and existence, of coffee smuggling, correlated with the difference in the coffee and free market exchange rates.

4. What *specific* export promotion policies should be adopted? Devaluation? Across the board subsidies? Selective devaluation? Selective subsidization? Or some other? All other things being equal, the Colombian government considers devaluation politically least desirable.

5. Regardless of what measures are decided upon, there will be serious problems of implementation. Consequently the government expects the recommendation to be quite specific (except possibly for coffee). Thus,

[2] Sheahan, John, "Imports, Investment and Growth—Colombia," *Development Policy: Theory and Practice,* Gustav F. Papanek, ed. (Cambridge: Harvard University Press, 1968), pp. 93–116.

[3] While the size of the coffee stock is a closely guarded secret, it is safe to say that it equals at least two to three years of production.

if the export promotion policy is to be selective, the criteria (or criterion) to be used to distinguish between activities and commodities should be clearly stated.

Table 5–1 *Excess of Colombian Domestic Prices Over International Prices[a]*

Sector	*Excess of Domestic over International Prices (Per cent)*
1. Agriculture	—
2. Mining and quarrying	—
3. Handicrafts	—
4. Food	30
5. Beverages	200
6. Tobacco	150
7. Textiles	50
8. Wood and cork	60
9. Furniture	100
10. Paper products	20
11. Printing	—
12. Leather and footwear	35
13. Rubber products	40
14. Chemicals	25
15. Coal and Petroleum products	—
16. Non-metallic mineral products	45
17. Basic metals	75
18. Metal products	90
19. Machinery, non-electrical	40
20. Machinery, electrical	40
21. Transport equipment	60
22. Other industries	90
23. Construction	—
24. Services	—

[a] The determination of the relation of domestic and international prices requires very careful survey work. In particular, product comparability and quality differences must be appropriately taken into account and raise special difficulties when imports competitive with domestic production are either very limited or entirely non-existent. Whereas empirical studies of this kind have been conducted in some countries (for example, Pakistan, Argentina, Israel), data for Colombia are not available. The figures given in this table represent an assumption based on what fragmentary information there is.

Case 6: Import Control Policy

While the Government of Colombia is cognizant of the fact that all possible measures to promote exports are necessary to help resolve the balance of payments disequilibrium, it has also become aware of the need to curtail imports to achieve a viable balance of payments equilibrium.

Early in 1967 the Government began to consider alternative import control policies. It was realized that any policy would have to be effective almost immediately. The exchange reserves had fallen from $215 million on December 31, 1959 to $77 million as of December 31, 1966, approximately equal to only one month of imports. A continued loss of reserves would make the implementation of a stabilization policy extremely difficult.

On the other hand, the Government considered it important that any import control policy be a flexible one because it was not clear whether the decline in export earnings was a permanent one. Given past behavior of exports, which exhibited considerable year to year variation, it was difficult to forecast the future trend with any degree of certainty. If the decline in export earnings was basically considered a short run phenomena, then it would be merely necessary to postpone imports from a period of scarce foreign exchange to a time when export earnings were rising again. A more comprehensive policy would be needed, however, if the decline in export earnings turned out to be of secular nature.

Should the decline in export earnings be indeed of a long run nature, so that any proposed import control policy would have to be in force for some time, it is important that the protection afforded under the import restrictions benefit "efficient" industries. Otherwise there will be a misallocation of resources which will hamper future export expansion. At the same time any import restrictions should minimize disincentives to exports. While it is probably impossible to avoid some rise in industrial costs after import controls have been imposed, it would be desirable if such cost increases have only a slight effect on export industries, existing or potential.

The Government, having recently instituted a series of measures designed to stabilize prices and bring the past inflationary trend under control, is anxious that the import policy not damage this effort unduly. Thus to avoid setting off a new price-wage spiral, it is desirable to adopt a policy that will bring about the smallest rise in the internal price level, both in terms of its initial impact as well as in terms of secondary price increases.

Special problems will arise in implementing import controls effectively. Colombia has a long and poorly guarded frontier with Venezuela, a country that enjoys a strong balance of payments position and hence has a liberal import policy. It is feared that as imports into Colombia become restricted, businessmen will find it profitable to smuggle in goods from Venezuela, thus nullifying the import policy. Hence some attempt should be made to devise a policy that will minimize the incentive to obtain imports illegally from Venezuela.

A number of secondary goals should also be taken into account in framing an import control policy. Income distribution should not become less egalitarian. On the contrary, if possible, the share of wages in national income should increase. At the same time, employment must be expanded.

Finally, in an economy marked by a high degree of monopoly and cartelization, any import policy should not strengthen such tendencies. If the increase in the price of imported goods is likely to produce windfall profits, such profits should be kept as low as possible.

The Government has considered a variety of instruments as possible components of an import restriction policy. The main ones are devaluation, an increase in import duties, imposition of import quotas, use of preimport deposits, reduction of domestic credit, reduction of government expenditures, and an increase in domestic taxation. Again, in framing an import policy it will be necessary to consider whether the measures to be used should apply to all imports or be used selectively. In the latter case a decision will have to be made as to which imports will be affected and how.

The Colombian Planning Commission therefore has to consider the following questions:

1. What will be the likely effect of each of the possible policy tools on the major and minor policy goals?

2. Since some tools will have a positive result by one criterion and a negative one by another, can a mix be devised that will yield a better result for a combination of objectives?

3. What policy should be recommended?

Case 7: Comprehensive Policy for the External Sector

The Colombian government recognizes that its export promotion and import control policies are not mutually independent. Success on the export side allows a more liberal import policy. However, the increase in exports will require an increase in imported raw materials and capital goods used in the manufacture of exportables. On the other hand, a rise in the price of imports increases the cost of production for export goods, reducing their competitiveness in the international market. Furthermore, the lack of certain imports may preclude some production for exports altogether. Finally, some policy measures directly affect both imports and exports—for example, devaluation.

In addition to the interdependence noted above, the government is concerned about the effect of its import and export policies on the balance of invisibles. Thus, each of the possible import control policies would have different effects on the inflow and outflow of foreign and domestic capital, as well as on the movement of tourists and earnings from other invisible items. The same can be said of the various export promotion measures.

The Colombian Planning Commission is thus requested to analyze the following points:

1. What are the effects of each export promotion policy alternative (Case 5) on imports?

2. What are the effects of each import control policy (Case 6) on exports?

3. Taking these interactions into account, what would be the best balance of trade policy?

4. What are the effects of each export promotion and import control measures on foreign investment in Colombia?

5. What are the likely effects on the flow of tourists? On other invisible items?

In view of the above, what would be the most desirable comprehensive policy from the point of view of the foreign sectors as a whole?

Fiscal and Monetary Policy

Introduction

Annual budgeting exercises are among the regular functions of governments. They are concerned with the government's own fiscal budget and with the management of the short term aggregate supply and demand balance.

Aggregate supply and demand in the economy must be managed to be consistent with the growth objectives and the objective of price stability. A failure in this respect affects the achievement of the growth target as well as in the first instance the balance of payments, employment, and the price level. The fiscal budget, in turn, has very specific effects on the services and investments government can provide, the distribution of income between different groups in the economy and the relative role of the government and private sectors.

Decisions on the budget, keeping in mind both narrower fiscal considerations and broader considerations of managing the economy require decisions on the creation of money, the raising of taxes, and the setting of the level of government expenditures.

A decision on the amount of money to create involves deciding on the extension of credit not only to government, but also to the private sector. It implies essentially a judgment on the behavior and the reactions of the latter. An increase in the money supply can increase demand or supply or both. Analysis—plus a good crystal ball—is required to predict its effects under particular circumstances. Does an increase in the availability of money and credit lead to an increase in private sector expenditure, or is such an extension of credit equivalent to pushing on a string? Conversely, does the increased desire to spend on the part of the private sector mean that there is an increased need for money in the form of transaction balances? Does the demand for money stem from the desire for credit to finance consumer durables or producer investment goods? Does an increase in output on the part of the private sector require an increase of credit and money balances to make it possbile to maintain inventories of goods in process? In short, is money primarily an element in the demand function of the private sector, or is it an element in the production function of the private sector; does it contribute to increased demand and therefore inflationary pressures, or does it contribute to increased supply and therefore deflationary pressures?

Furthermore, does an increase of credit to the private sector lead to an increase in tax revenue (collections) and therefore improvement in the government budget (cash) situation, or does it lead to an increased demand for government services and therefore to an increase in government expenditure? And how does an increase in credit to the private sector affect the willingness of that sector to hold government financial paper of one sort or another?

In turn, how does the government fiscal balance affect the behavior of the private sector? Does an increase in government investment lead to increased output in the private sector through the improvement of the infrastructure? Or does it compete with private investment by pre-empting the capacity to supply goods and services from the construction and other capital goods industries? Does government consumption contribute to aggregate demand in the economy and thus insure a high level of output, or does it pre-empt supply of consumption goods and imports and thus prevent the private sector from acquiring commodities it would otherwise desire to buy? Does an increase in taxation affect private consumption or private savings and, if the latter, what is the impact on government borrowing or private investment? Furthermore, what impact does it have on the private demand for credit?

The budgeting procedures, both from the aggregate national and from the fiscal point of view must take into account this complex of interrelationships. Decisions depend on some judgment of which are preponderant, how they interact and over what time period. Otherwise, the objectives of growth, stability, and balance of payments equilibrium will not be achieved.

Finally, if a country is faced with a structural balance of payments deficit and decides to devalue, a whole set of new budgeting problems arise. The level at which the new exchange rate(s) is (or are) fixed obviously influences the impact of the devaluation on the domestic price level as well as on the aggregate supply and demand schedules. Furthermore, the effectiveness of any devaluation will not be independent of actions on fiscal and monetary policy. It is possible to argue that devaluation will increase the revenue of exporters and therefore contribute to inflationary pressures in the economy which must in turn be offset by tight fiscal and monetary policy. On the other hand, it can be argued that a devaluation will produce an increase in the domestic price level and therefore also an increase in the requirement for transaction balances of the private sector. In consequence an easy monetary policy would be indicated. On the strictly fiscal side it can be argued that devaluation will increase the tax base and therefore government revenues. One can also argue, however, that devaluation will increase the cost of government operations and therefore its expenditures. The net balance of these two effects will obviously be reflected in a new budget surplus or deficit which in turn will have an impact on the functioning of the private sector.

Short term macro policy therefore requires first analysing the likely effects of various policy tools in isolation and then devising a policy package which will best achieve some major objectives at not too great a cost in terms of other objectives.

Suggested Readings on Fiscal and Monetary Policy

The student is expected to be familiar with starred (*) items.

Monetary Budgeting

1. *Ahrensdorf, Joachim, and Kanesathesan, S. "Variations in the Money Multiplier and Their Implication for Central Banking." *I.M.F. Staff Papers,* vol. 8, Nov. 1960, pp. 126–150.

2. Triffin, Robert. "A Simplified Scheme for the Integration of Monetary and Income Analysis." Memoria, V Reunion de Tecnicos de los Bancos Centrales del Continente Americano, Banco de la Republica, Bogota, 1957, pp. 293–311.

3. Brovedani, Bruno. "The Use of Banking Statistics as a Guide to Monetary Policies in Latin America." Ibid., pp. 117–137.

4. I.M.F., Statistical Division. "The Monetary Surveys in International Financial Statistics." Ibid., pp. 165–181.

5. Goode, Richard, and Thorn, Richard J. "Variable Reserve Requirements Against Commercial Bank Deposits." *I.M.F. Staff Papers,* vol. 7, April 1959, pp. 9–45.

6. *Knight, Harold M. "A Monetary Budget." *I.M.F. Staff Papers,* vol. 7, Oct. 1959, pp. 210–223.

Monetary Analysis

7. Polak, J. J. "Monetary Analysis of Income Formation and Payments Problems." *I.M.F. Staff Papers,* vol. 6, Nov. 1957, pp. 1–50.

8. *———, and Boissonneault, Lorette. "Monetary Analysis of Income and Imports and its Statistical Application." *I.M.F. Staff Papers,* vol. 7, April 1960, pp. 349–415.

9. Fleming, J. Marcus, and Boissonneault, Lorette. "Money Supply and Imports." *I.M.F. Staff Papers,* vol. 8, May 1961, pp. 227–240.

10. Prais, S. J. "Some Mathematical Notes on the Quantity Theory of Money in an Open Economy." *I.M.F. Staff Papers,* vol. 8, May 1961, pp. 212–226.

11. Tsiang, S. C. "Liquidity Preference and Loanable Funds Theories, Multiplier and Velocity Analyses: A Synthesis." *American Economic Review,* vol. 46, Sept. 1956, pp. 539–564, especially Section IV.

12. Kanesathasan, S. "Government Imports and Import Taxes in Monetary Analysis of Income and Imports." *I.M.F. Staff Papers,* Dec. 1961, pp. 412–426.

13. Argy, Victor. "Monetary Variables and the Balance of Payments." *I.M.F. Staff Papers,* vol. 16, no. 2, July 1969, pp. 267–288.

Taxation and Fiscal Policy

14. *Bird, Richard. "Optimal Tax Policy for a Developing Country: The Case of Colombia." *Finanz Archiv,* vol. 29, Feb. 1970, pp. 30–53.

15. *Musgrave, Richard, et al. *Fiscal Reform for Colombia: The Final Report and Staff Papers for Colombian Commission for Tax Reform.* Edited by Malcolm Gillis. Cambridge: International Tax Program, 1970, chapters I, II, III.

16. Martin, A., and Lewis, W. Arthur. "Patterns of Public Revenue and Expenditure." *Manchester School of Economic and Social Studies,* vol. 24, September 1956, pp. 203–232. Reprinted in Bird, Richard, and Oldman, Oliver. *Readings on Taxation in Developing Countries.* Baltimore: Johns Hopkins Press, 1967.

17. Musgrave, R. A. "Estimating the Distribution of the Tax Burden." Joint Tax Program OAS/IDB/ECLA, *Problems of Tax Administration in Latin America.* Baltimore: Johns Hopkins Press, 1965, chapter 2. See also Comments by F. J. Hershel and J. A. Pechman.

18. Crockett, J. P. "Common Obstacles to Effective Tax Administration in Latin America." Joint Tax Program OAS/IDB/ECLA, *Problems of Tax Administration in Latin America.* Baltimore: Johns Hopkins Press, 1965, chapter 1.

19. Musgrave, R. A. *Fiscal Systems.* New Haven and London: Yale University Press 1969, chapters 3, 4, 5, 6, 8, 13.

Inflation, Devaluation and Stabilization

20. Oliveira Campos, Roberto de. "Two Views on Inflation in Latin America." Edited by A. O. Hirschman. *Latin American Issues,* pp. 69–80.

21. Felix, David. "An Alternative View of the 'Monetarist'—'Structuralist' Controversy." Ibid., pp. 81–94.

22. Hirschman, A. O. "Inflation in Chile." *Journeys Towards Progress,* chapter 3, pp. 215–289.

23. Harberger, Arnold. "The Dynamics of Inflation in Chile" in Carl F. Christ et al. *Measurement in Economics: Studies in Mathematical Economics and Econometrics.*

24. *Baer, Werner. "The Inflation Controversy in Latin America: A Survey." *Latin American Research Review,* vol. 2, no. 2, Winter 1967.

25. Lewis, W. Arthur. "Closing Remarks." Edited by Baer, W., and Kerstenetzky, Isaac. *Inflation and Growth in Latin America.* Homewood, Ill.: Richard D. Irwin, 1964, pp. 21–33.

26. Maynard, Geoffrey, and Van Rijckeghem, Willy. "Stabilization Policy in an Inflationary Economy." Edited by G. F. Papanek, *Development Policy: Theory and Practice.* Harvard University Press 1968, pp. 207–235.

27. Eshag, Eprime, and Thorp, Rosemary. "Economic and Social Consequences of Orthodox Economic Policies in Argentina in the Post-War Years." *Bulletin of the Oxford University Institute of Statistics,* vol. 27, no. 1, Feb. 1965.

28. *Meade, J. E. *The Theory of International Trade: The Balance of Payments,* vol. 1. London: Oxford University Press, 1960, chps. IX, "Financial Policy for Internal and External Balance," X, "Conflicts between Internal and External Balance," XI, "Price Adjustments as a Means of Policy."

29. *Machlup, F. "Relative Prices and Aggregate Spending in the Analysis of Devaluation." *The American Economic Review,* vol. 14, June 1955, pp. 255–278.

30. *Fleming, J. M. "Exchange Depreciation, Financial Policy and the Domestic Price Level." *I.M.F. Staff Papers,* vol. 6, April 1958, pp. 289–322.

31. *Cohen, B. "Measuring the Short Run Impact of a Country's Import Restrictions on its Exports." *The Quarterly Journal of Economics,* vol. 80, August 1966, pp. 456–462.

32. *Balassa, Bela. "The Purchasing Power Parity Doctrine: A Reappraisal." *The Journal of Political Economy,* vol. 72, December 1964, pp. 584–596.

33. *Orcutt, G. H. "Measurement of Price Elasticity in International Trade." *The Review of Economics and Statistics,* vol. 32, May 1950, pp. 117–132.

34. *Houthakker, H., and Magee, Stephen P. "Income and Price Elasticities in World Trade." *The Review of Economics and Statistics,* vol. 51, May 1969, pp. 111–125.

35. Mallon, Richard D. "Exchange Policy-Argentina." Edited by G. F. Papanek. *Development Policy: Theory and Practice.* Harvard University Press 1968, pp. 175–206.

36. ———. "Balance of Payments Adjustment in a Semi-Industrialized Agricultural Export Economy: The Argentine Case." Economic Development Report 109. Cambridge: Development Advisory Service, 1968.

Country Background: Peru

Peru has an area of approximately 500,000 square miles and a population of about twelve million. The country is divided into three fairly clear geographic regions: a thin coastal strip averaging some 30 to 50 miles in width, a Sierra region comprising the Andean chain and inter-Andean plateau, and a jungle region, the Amazonic plain in the east of the country. The coastal region is a natural desert traversed by approximately two dozen short rivers which form the basis of an extensive irrigation system supporting a predominantly industrial agriculture. The Northern and Central coast produce long-staple cotton and sugar for export and rice and other food stuffs for domestic consumption. The Southern coast produces mainly food stuffs. The Sierra is basically a region of mines and subsistence agriculture, though some agricultural products are transported to the urban areas of the coast. The jungle region is very undeveloped and produces mainly timber and other jungle products. Manufacturing industry is concentrated on the coast, in particular in the area of the capital city of Lima and its port, Callao.

Peru's history conditions its current reality. In pre-Columbian days Peru was the heartland of the Inca empire, which achieved a high level of sophistication in administrative and economic organization. The Inca communal farming institution called "Ayllu" survives in parts of the Sierra where land is still held and farmed in common. The descendants of the Inca population today constitute more than one half of all Peruvians. The Spanish conquest and colonial domination, lasting 300 years, gave Peru most of its current cultural traditions, including the bases of its present land holding and water rights system. Independence was declared in 1821 and conclusively achieved on the battlefield in 1824.[1]

Economic Structure and Performance

Taken as a whole, the period 1950–65 has been one of rapid and sustained growth.[2] Measured at constant prices, the GNP of 1965 was more than two and one-third times that of 1950, which means that growth reached an average annual rate of 5.6 per cent. Despite the substantial increase in the population, real GNP per capita grew in the same period by 56 per cent, in other words, at a rate of three per cent a year. There have been no important fluctuations in this growth trend except a marked reduction in the years 1956–59 during which there was no growth in real per capita terms. The year to year fluctuations must be attributed mainly to the

[1] For a detailed account of Peru's republican history see Fredrick B. Pike, *The Modern History of Peru* (New York: Praeger, 1967).

[2] The following survey abstracts the Introductory Summary of "Cuentas Nacionales del Peru, 1950–65" (Lima: Banco Central de Reserva de Peru, 1966).

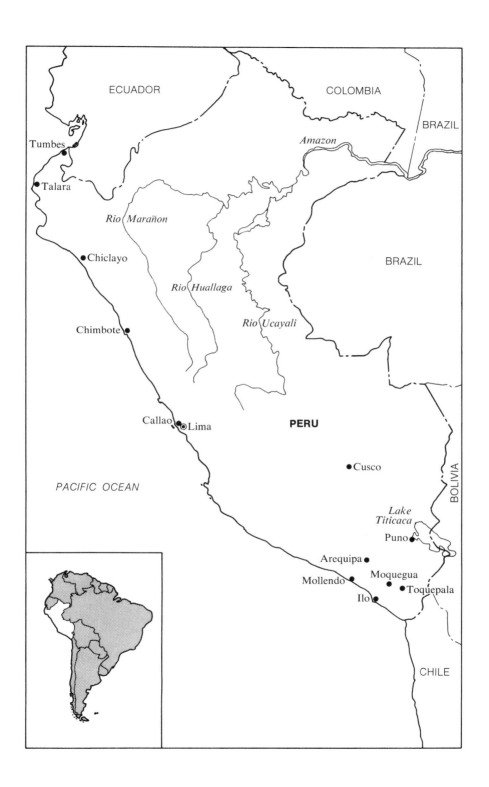

short run instability of export earnings and of agricultural production. On the basis of five year periods, the average annual rate of growth of GNP was 6 per cent from 1950 to 1955, 4.3 per cent from 1955 to 1960, 6.6 per cent from 1960 to 1965. If the per capita figure is analyzed, growth was higher in the first five year period since at that time population grew at only an average of 2 per cent compared with 2.6 per cent for the period 1950–65 as a whole and 3 per cent in 1960–65.

The rates of growth of gross national product and national income during this period have been among the highest for any of the Latin American countries. During almost all of these years the national economic policy that was followed made possible two important achievements: a favorable behavior of investment and an extraordinary growth of exports. Despite this economic progress there are still important problems to be solved. If we remember that in 1965 GNP per capita was only 9,763 soles (U.S. $364), it becomes evident that a large part of the population still has low levels of income and consumption. The regional income distribution is extremely skewed and the differences between the groups that receive the income appear to be considerable even in areas of relative prosperity. The dynamic sector of the economy was concentrated on the Coast, in particular in the zone of Lima and Callao.

The majority of the population has benefited from the increase in national product and income; thus, from 1950 to 1963 average salaries and wages rose in real terms by 4 per cent and 3.5 per cent per year respectively.[3] Wage and salary earners are about half the labor force and, in turn, receive almost half the national income. The real income of artisans, businessmen, professionals and other individual, nonagricultural, workers has risen at similar rates.

The significant increase in the standard of living has had its major exception among the independent farmers (self-employment in agriculture). Those workers, in a majority owners of small family units, are approximately one third of the labor force and produce practically at a subsistence level. Their real income seems to have grown at rates substantially below average.

The functional income distribution has changed somewhat as a result of different rates of growth in average incomes and of changes in the structure of the labor force. The most important of these changes has been the reduction in the participation of the independent farmers in national income from 22 per cent in 1950 to 12 per cent in 1963. That reduction reflects not only the slower growth of their average income, but also the emigration of the farmers to other sectors. Although the number of independent farmers has grown by 15 per cent since 1950, the rest of the labor force has grown

---

[3] Peru's legal system distinguishes between personnel hired on a monthly basis (empleados) and those hired on a daily basis (obreros). The former's income is called salary (sueldo) and the latter's called wage (salario).

during the same period by more than 50 per cent. Nonagricultural self-employed persons, in turn, have continued to receive approximately 15 per cent of the national income. The share of wage and salary earnings shows a substantial increase—from 39 per cent in 1950 to 48 per cent in 1963—which in large part corresponds to the reduction in the participation of the independent farmers. Taken in conjunction, the three types of income that wholly or mainly represent return to labor received nearly 75 per cent of the national income, in 1950 as well as in 1963.

Among the types of income that represent mainly return to property, there has been a change in the component of rent which fell from eight per cent in 1950 to six per cent in 1963. The main part of that kind of income consists of the return which is imputed to owner occupied housing, which means that it is distributed very widely among the population. During the whole period the share of profit and interest stayed approximately constant around 18 per cent of national income. About one-third of that income was absorbed by the government through the profits' tax, another one-third was reinvested directly by the firms, and the remaining one-third, that is, between five and six per cent of national income, was distributed to the owners as dividends.

The growth of the economy has been accompanied by changes in its sectoral structure. These changes have primarily consisted of an important reduction in the contribution of agriculture and the corresponding increase in the importance of other sectors. Thus, from 1950 to 1963 the contribution of agriculture to national income fell from 35 per cent to 22 per cent. If fishing is excluded the reduction is even greater, from 35 per cent to 20 per cent. At the same time the contribution of manufacturing industry rose from 15 per cent to 17 per cent, that of commerce from 11 per cent to 16 per cent and that of government from 7 to 10 per cent. The contribution of mining stayed constant around five per cent.

Within each sector important changes have also taken place. Thus the contribution of fishing to the total of agricultural income grew from less than 2 per cent in 1950 to 11 per cent in 1964. In mining, iron ore and copper grew more than the other products, especially oil. Iron ore, the extraction of which began in 1953, amounted by 1964 to 11 per cent of the total mining production; and copper, which in 1950 represented 12 per cent, contributed 30 per cent in 1964.

Agriculture is still the main source of income as can be seen from the fact that in 1965 one-half the families of the country were directly dependent upon it for their subsistence. However, the productivity of that labor is extemely low. These two characteristics of the economy are closely related to the low level of the average national income.

The rates of growth of the real product show substantial differences among sectors. From 1950 to 1964 value added in agriculture grew on the average by 4.6 per cent, somewhat less than the 5.7 per cent of total GNP.

Within this sector, fishing grew rapidly at an average annual rate of 19.5 per cent whereas the narrowly defined agricultural and forestry production grew only at 3.8 per cent. The statistical evidence on the production of food is somewhat questionable but it appears to indicate that in the period under review the national production of food grew approximately at the rate of increase of demand. Three other sectors increased at a particularly rapid rate in the period 1950–64: manufacturing at a rate of 7.8 per cent per year, mining at a similar rate and electricity at 8.8 per cent per year.

In large part the growth of the total real product has been due to improvements in productivity. It is estimated that the output per worker grew at an average annual rate of 3.5 per cent for the economy as a whole; more rapidly in mining and manufacturing (5.4 per cent and 5.1 per cent respectively), but also in agriculture where productivity increased at an average of 3.4 per cent a year. This improvement in agriculture made it possible to shift part of the labor force to other sectors such as trade and services, which have a higher productivity in absolute terms but a lower rate of growth of productivity.

On the average the prices of the goods and services comprised in the GNP rose at the annual rate of something more than eight per cent during the whole period. This increase was never less than 3.4 per cent per year and during three two-year periods (1950–51, 1959–60, and 1964–65) the rate exceeded 10 per cent. The highest yearly price increases were observed in 1964 (12 per cent) and 1965 (15 per cent).

Apparently, the inflation in the two-year periods mentioned above originated in the exceptional expansion of bank credit which in turn was caused mainly by Central Reserve Bank financing of the government deficit. Since the exchange rate increased relatively less than the domestic price level, prices of imports showed a lower increase than those of domestic products and contributed to dampening the total price increase. Furthermore, it is important to note that the price of food appears not to have had a major impact on the inflation since it did not increase by more than the general GNP price index. The major price increases occurred in construction, the cost of which grew at an annual average rate of 10.5 per cent.

Savings and Investment

Peru's high rate of investment has been an important factor in the rapid growth of the economy. On the average, gross investment represented 25 per cent of GNP during the period and in no year did that percentage fall below 18 per cent. The rate of formation of capital was higher during 1952–53 and 1956–58 as a result of the large investments in mining. Investment fell especially during the years in which there was uncertainty or fluctuation in the exchange rate, such as 1954 and 1959, but in each case it recovered rapidly to its previous levels. Nearly one-half the investment during the period consisted of new construction.

Investment of the public sector has grown rapidly in recent years. A large part of it (12 per cent of gross domestic investment during the years 1960–65) was chanelled through independent public corporations that operate in the business field. During this time, the investment of the public sector as a whole—including that undertaken directly by the central government and local governments—represented 19% of total investment.

A substantial part of gross capital formation, more than 40 per cent, was financed directly by the business sector from its retained earnings and depreciation allowances. Personal savings contributed one-third of total savings. Furthermore, there has been a net capital inflow from abroad which consisted mainly of loans to the public sector and provided something more than a tenth of the savings available for domestic investment. The remainder of savings was supplied from the surplus on current account of the central and local governments.

The Foreign Sector

Exports have played a key role in the growth of the national product. The exports of goods and services estimated for 1965 are more than three times the size of those of 1950, which yields one of the highest growth rates of the components of GNP. This rapid expansion of exports—which has contributed to an increase of foreign exchange inflow at an average rate of 8.9 per cent per year—has been concentrated in new products, especially fish and its subproducts, iron ore, and coffee, all of which, taken together, were less than 4 per cent of total exports in 1950 while reaching 39 per cent in 1965. The main fluctuations in this upward trend of exports took place in two periods. The first of these, spanning 1950–53 showed a considerable price increase initially, due to the Korean War. However, prices fell again later with a consequent reduction of export receipts which in 1953 were only 88 per cent of the 1951 level. The second period, from 1959 to 1962, saw exports rising by two-thirds due in part to an improvement of international prices but mainly due to the considerable growth in volume.

The terms of trade had an important effect on the foreign exchange receipts at certain times during the period, but in general they showed little net change. From 1950 to 1959, export prices rose less than import prices and the terms of trade (in soles) measured by the relationship between the implicit deflators of exports and imports showed a deterioration of 25 per cent. By contrast, from 1959 to 1965, the tendency of prices was the converse and as a result the terms of trade improved by 38 per cent. The net result of these changes has been that in 1965 the terms of trade were at the same level as in 1950. Therefore, the real GNP adjusted to reflect the terms of trade, which includes the changes due to variations in the foreign purchasing power of the country, grew in this period at an average rate similar to the unadjusted GNP.

The rapid expansion of exports also influenced the growth of the national economy by strengthening the capacity to import. Of this substantial increase in the goods and services acquired abroad, about a third constituted investment goods. It is important to note that despite the important devaluations of the national currency which took place in 1953–54 and 1958–59, the soles cost of imports only doubled (and in fact decreased somewhat after 1959) whereas domestic prices rose by a factor of three. This relative cheapening of foreign products probably has stimulated domestic investment since the import content of investment is much greater than that of consumption.

Finally, the strong growth of exports permitted the accumulation of dollar and foreign exchange reserves within the free exchange rate system in force, which contributed to creating a climate of confidence among local and foreign investors.

The Role of the Government

The government played an increasingly important role during the period. It absorbed a growing proportion of the national product and used these revenues to increase its share of the final expenditure on GNP and to subsidize in ever increasing proportion the operating expenditures and investment of the enterprises of the "Independent Public Subsector."

The tax burden, measured by the coefficient of total taxes to GNP, rose from 11 to 15 per cent in the period 1950 to 1965. Much of that increase came from indirect taxes on business which rose from one-third of the total taxation to two-thirds, due to increases in the two main types of indirect taxes: import duties and taxes on domestic transactions. Personal taxes are not high, in 1965, some 15 per cent of tax collections, with two-thirds of this amount representing contributions to the social security system. Taxes on profits provided another 18 per cent and in great part were paid by producers of goods for export.

The growth of tax revenues has been faster than that of the government's purchases of goods and services, since an increasing part of the revenue has been transferred to households and corporations. From 1952 to 1965 the size of these transfers, mainly pensions, contributions to social security and subsidies to state enterprises, has increased from less than one-fourth to nearly one-third of total government expenditure.

The percentage of GNP represented by the purchase of goods and services on the part of the government rose from 8 per cent to 12 per cent during the period. Government wages represented the greatest part of consumption expenditures and at present are almost equal to one-half of the total government expenditures. Investment also fluctuated from year to year, but on the average has been 13 per cent of the total. The revenue from taxation has also financed investment, to the extent that the subsidies given to public enterprise have been used to finance capital items. The participation of the local governments in public sector finance has been small. In 1963, municipalities and districts represented only five per cent of total government expenditure. Wages and salaries absorbed one-half of that amount and investment one-sixth. Indirect taxes and personal taxes are the main sources of revenue for these sectors of government since they do not collect taxes on profits.

Development Strategy

Peru's economic policy has traditionally been one of relying on private enterprise and the market system to generate growth.[3] The Government has provided infrastructure and tax incentives but relatively little direct entrepreneurship. Recent policy has aimed at expansion and diversification of exports, a moderate amount of import substitution and a large increase in social services and infrastructure. Import duties have been progressively raised but the free exchange market has been preserved and price stability has been regarded as a policy goal. For the medium term, no change in these policy lines is expected.

Table Pr.–1   *Gross National Product 1950–1966*

Year	GNP (Current Prices) (in millions of soles)	Prices (Implicit Deflator)	Real GNP (1963 Prices) (in millions of soles)	Population (Thousands)	Real GNP Per Capita (1963 Soles)
1950	15,577	40.0	38,956	8,069.5	4,828
1951	19,746	45.9	43,036	8,218.3	5,237
1952	21,021	47.5	44,285	8,368.2	5,292
1953	22,673	50.1	45,247	8,525.9	5,307
1954	26,302	53.0	49,613	8,697.9	5,704
1955	28,947	55.6	52,065	8,890.8	5,856
1956	32,385	59.5	54,439	9,105.0	5,979
1957	35,535	64.6	54,968	9,336.1	5,888
1958	39,549	69.6	56,819	9,583.6	5,929
1959	46,260	78.6	58,834	9,846.9	5,975
1960	55,518	86.5	64,175	10,125.4	6,338
1961	62,294	89.7	69,411	10,420.4	6,661
1962	71,700	94.5	75,836	10,732.3	7,066
1963	78,710	100.0	78,710	11,059.2	7,117
1964	94,994	113.0	84,098	11,359.2	7,404
1965	113,000	128.1	88,146	11,750.4	7,502
1966	134,016	143.8	93,186	12,103.0	7,699

Source: Banco Central de Reserva del Peru, *Cuentas Nacionales del Peru* 1950–1967 (1968) 1950–1965 (1966), Table 1.

[3] This section is written from the perspective of 1966, the time setting of the following cases.

Table Pr.–2 Real Gross National Product by Type of Expenditure, 1950–1966

	1950	1951	1952	1953	1954	1955	1956	1957	1958
					(millions of 1963 soles)				
Personal Consumption	27,605	29,142	28,735	29,471	35,090	37,424	37,504	37,908	39,826
Government Consumption	3,860	4,465	4,618	4,962	4,976	5,051	5,473	5,429	5,511
Gross Investment	7,942	11,227	12,780	12,757	10,230	12,365	14,858	16,220	13,888
Machinery & Equipment	3,147	4,355	4,890	5,215	3,830	4,099	6,245	7,018	5,777
New Construction	3,900	4,948	5,810	6,346	5,276	6,316	7,203	7,432	6,806
Inventory Increase	895	1,924	2,080	1,196	1,124	1,950	1,410	1,770	1,305
Exports of Goods & Services	5,915	6,096	6,856	7,390	8,003	8,634	9,357	9,655	9,935
Imports of Goods & Services	6,366	7,894	8,704	9,333	8,686	11,409	12,753	14,244	12,341
GNP	38,956	43,036	44,285	45,247	49,613	52,065	54,439	54,968	56,819
GNP Adjusted to Reflect Changes in the Terms of Trade	39,802	44,889	44,847	45,247	49,709	52,324	54,832	55,325	55,706

Table Pr.–2 (continued)

	1959	1960	1961	1962	1963	1964	1965	1966
					(millions of 1963 soles)			
Personal Consumption	42,322	43,154	45,949	51,405	57,117	60,519	64,554	69,485
Government Consumption	5,568	6,111	7,037	7,361	7,714	8,865	9,685	9,571
Gross Investment	10,505	13,682	15,588	17,288	16,391	17,131	19,425	23,755
Machinery & Equipment	5,055	5,482	7,083	8,676	9,051	8,269	9,982	11,443
New Construction	4,875	5,210	6,452	6,962	6,060	6,394	7,540	8,286
Inventory Increase	575	2,990	2,053	1,650	1,280	2,468	1,903	4,026
Exports of Goods & Services	11,292	14,195	16,567	17,556	16,897	18,225	18,422	18,579
Imports of Goods & Services	10,853	12,967	15,730	17,774	19,409	20,642	23,940	28,204
GNP	58,834	64,175	69,411	75,836	78,710	84,098	88,146	93,186
GNP Adjusted to Reflect Changes in the Terms of Trade	57,253	62,997	67,771	74,748	78,710	86,741	90,272	98,069

Source: Banco Central de Reserva del Peru, *Cuentas Nacionales del Peru* 1950–1967 (1968); 1950–1965 (1966)

Table Pr.–3 National Income by Sector of Origin (Millions of soles)

	1950	1951	1952	1953	1954	1955	1956	1957	1958
Agriculture, forestry and fishing	5,004	6,702	6,703	6,916	7,761	8,134	8,253	8,697	9,947
Agriculture and forestry	4,916	6,607	6,598	6,794	7,629	7,973	8,044	8,503	9,553
Fishing	88	95	105	122	132	161	209	194	394
Mining and quarrying	659	1,245	1,020	987	1,214	1,287	1,429	1,474	1,147
Manufacturing	2,099	2,369	2,512	2,622	3,643	3,947	4,238	5,045	5,756
Construction	465	522	568	678	835	969	1,095	1,189	1,583
Electricity, gas and water	62	80	92	102	122	136	158	209	220
Transport, warehousing and communications	563	612	667	760	1,008	1,176	1,409	1,463	1,659
Commerce	1,625	1,793	2,177	2,410	2,356	2,854	3,652	3,852	3,941
Banking, insurance and real estate	331	402	487	566	610	661	826	1,018	1,135
Housing	1,115	1,291	1,462	1,612	1,702	1,867	2,013	2,300	2,591
Government	953	1,316	1,418	1,535	1,633	1,772	2,233	2,382	2,780
Services	1,319	1,451	1,617	1,890	2,433	2,804	3,255	3,681	4,327
National Income	14,195	17,783	18,723	20,078	23,317	25,607	28,561	31,310	35,086

Table Pr.–3 (continued)

	1959	1960	1961	1962	1963	1964	1965	1966
Agriculture, forestry and fishing	10,808	12,254	13,760	15,010	14,764	17,133	19,412	22,421
Agriculture and forestry	10,241	11,503	12,897	13,538	13,422	15,489	17,501	20,069
Fishing	567	751	863	1,472	1,342	1,644	1,911	2,352
Mining and quarrying	1,885	3,083	3,093	3,171	3,383	4,739	5,860	8,112
Manufacturing	6,998	8,281	9,359	10,918	11,146	13,308	15,166	16,869
Construction	1,797	1,966	2,144	2,551	2,772	3,716	4,693	5,400
Electricity, gas and water	251	303	346	447	553	611	866	1,207
Transport, warehousing and communications	1,838	2,051	2,311	2,770	3,002	3,771	4,330	4,936
Commerce	4,441	5,871	6,665	8,596	11,030	12,689	14,450	17,296
Banking, insurance and real estate	1,307	1,367	1,561	2,167	2,449	2,461	2,877	3,322
Housing	3,062	3,457	3,819	4,052	4,253	4,732	5,583	6,144
Government	3,499	3,898	4,796	5,563	6,562	8,521	10,569	12,715
Services	4,814	5,635	5,833	6,786	7,543	9,497	12,005	14,333
National Income	40,700	48,166	53,687	62,031	67,457	81,178	95,811	112,755

Source: Banco Central de Reserva del Peru, *Cuentas Nacionales del Peru*, 1950–1967 (1968), 1950–1965 (1966) Table 4.

Table Pr.–4 *The Growth of Manufacturing, 1963–1966*

Industry	Percentage Share of 1963 Value Added	Indices of Real Growth (1963 = 100)		
		1964	1965	1966
All Foods	30.2	112.8	107.2	118.2
Fishmeal	9.3	137.2	110.6	126.8
Sugar & Sub-Products	8.6	94.1	93.0	100.6
Other Food Industries	12.3	107.4	114.5	123.9
Textiles	12.5	100.7	121.7	122.7
Chemicals	9.1	112.0	125.8	142.4
Basic Metals	8.9	103.7	105.2	101.2
Beverage	7.9	104.4	123.3	157.4
Mechanical	7.7	104.8	117.4	130.1
Shoes & Apparel	5.0	111.7	120.2	134.0
Non-Metallic	4.6	115.1	132.2	149.3
Others	14.1	110.8	132.8	146.0
Total	100.0	108.9	118.0	129.6

Source: INPI, quoted in Banco Central de Reserva del Peru, "Reseña Economica y Finacniera" Second Trimestr 1968.

Table Pr.–5 *Exchange Rate (Annual Average)*

Year	Exchange Rate
1950	15.43
1951	15.18
1952	15.55
1953	16.94
1954	19.69
1955	19.18
1956	19.23
1957	19.07
1958	23.40
1959	27.64
1960	27.30
1961	26.81
1962	26.81
1963	26.82
1964	26.82
1965	26.82
1966	26.82

Source: Boletín, Banco Central de Reserva del Peru, Junio de 1968, p. 28.

Table Pr.–6 Prices 1950–1966, GNP Sectoral Deflators

	1950	1951	1952	1953	1954	1955	1956	1957	1958
Personal Consumption Expenditure	41.8	46.6	50.9	53.9	55.4	58.1	61.1	66.7	72.7
Government Consumption Expenditure	29.3	36.0	36.4	39.9	41.6	44.3	54.0	57.6	63.6
Gross Investment	34.3	40.4	42.7	46.7	50.8	53.8	58.0	62.5	73.4
Machinery & Equipment	41.9	46.8	48.8	53.3	59.0	60.0	63.6	67.0	80.5
New Construction	26.1	31.0	34.6	39.9	43.0	48.0	52.3	57.1	67.1
Exports of Goods & Services	55.0	70.0	61.8	58.8	68.0	69.0	72.5	73.8	78.3
Imports of Goods & Services	48.1	53.7	57.1	58.8	67.2	67.0	69.6	71.2	88.2
Implicit GNP Deflator	40.0	45.9	47.5	50.1	53.0	55.6	59.5	64.6	69.6

Table Pr.–6 (continued)

	1959	1960	1961	1962	1963	1964	1965	1966
Personal Consumption Expenditure	81.0	89.0	93.5	96.4	100.0	109.8	127.9	139.2
Government Consumption Expenditure	75.4	78.2	84.4	92.0	100.0	115.2	129.5	154.6
Gross Investment	85.2	89.8	91.2	96.7	100.0	104.7	109.4	114.7
Machinery & Equipment	93.0	96.5	97.7	98.9	100.0	101.9	104.0	107.1
New Construction	76.7	81.6	83.3	94.2	100.0	108.9	117.1	124.4
Exports of Goods & Services	89.6	94.9	92.6	95.1	100.0	113.0	112.4	130.9
Imports of Goods & Services	104.2	103.5	102.8	101.4	100.0	98.7	101.0	104.0
Implicit GNP Deflator	78.6	86.5	89.7	94.5	100.0	113.0	128.1	143.8

Source: Table 9, *Cuentas Nacionales del Peru*, 1950–1967, 1950–1965.

Table Pr.–7 *Cost of Living Index For Lima, 1934–36 Expenditure Weights*

1950	481.5
1951	530.2
1952	567.0
1953	618.5
1954	651.9
1955	682.6
1956	719.9
1957	773.2
1958	834.6
1959	940.6
1960	1,021.8
1961	1,068.2
1962	1,138.4
1963	1,210.8
1964	1,337.9
1965	1,565.6
1966	1,766.0

Source: Boletin del Banco Central de Reserva del Peru, Lima, Junio de 1968, p. 27.

Table Pr.–8 *Cost of Living Index for Lima and Callao, 1960 Expenditure Weights*

	Food	Housing	Clothing	Furniture	Various	Total
	(*Blue & White Collar Workers*)					
1961	107	104	107	105	101	106.0
1962	112	105	114	110	105	113.0
1963	120	107	123	115	109	119.8
1964	135	109	145	130	121	131.6
1965	159	124	160	151	143	153.2
1966	175	134	175	168	157	166.8
	(*Blue Collar Workers*)					
1961	108	104	107	105	101	106.8
1962	114	105	114	110	105	113.8
1963	123	108	123	115	109	121.0
1964	138	110	147	130	120	133.7
1965	164	126	162	152	142	156.3
1966	182	137	177	168	156	171.1
	(*White Collar Workers*)					
1961	105	103	107	105	101	104.5
1962	109	104	115	110	105	111.1
1963	116	106	123	116	110	117.2
1964	129	108	143	129	123	127.6
1965	151	119	156	150	145	146.4
1966	163	128	170	167	160	158.2

Source: Boletin del Banco Central de Reserva del Peru, Lima, Junio de 1968.

Table Pr.-9 *Balance of Payments—1950–1966*

	1950	1951	1952	1953	1954	1955	1956	1957	1958
				(millions of dollars)					
A. Goods & Services	16.2	1.7	-47.0	-69.4	-18.0	-88.8	-110.0	-160.8	-138.0
Exports F.O.B.	198.4	259.1	245.7	228.3	254.3	281.2	320.2	331.5	291.8
Imports F.O.B.	149.3	223.0	257.2	257.5	225.4	294.6	342.4	402.1	344.7
Balance of Trade	49.1	36.1	-11.5	-29.2	28.9	-13.4	-22.2	-70.6	-52.9
Freight & Insurance on Goods	-12.4	-21.0	-25.7	-31.3	-23.5	-35.5	-44.2	-45.6	-42.2
Investment Income	-20.6	-13.5	-10.6	-12.2	-24.0	-38.2	-36.8	-34.2	-36.2
Other Services	0.1	0.1	0.8	3.3	0.6	-1.7	-6.8	-10.4	-6.7
Exports of Goods & Services	217.3	282.6	274.0	257.0	280.8	313.2	356.4	374.8	332.7
Imports of Goods & Services	199.6	279.5	319.6	324.9	296.8	398.6	482.4	531.9	466.8
B. Transfer Payments	1.3	1.4	3.7	4.8	7.8	7.7	11.3	17.5	14.7
C. Balance on Current Account (A + B)	17.5	3.1	-43.3	-64.6	-10.2	-81.1	-98.7	-143.3	-123.3
D. Long Term Private Capital	-8.0	22.0	34.7	50.4	-13.8	7.1	50.0	98.9	89.3
Direct Foreign Investment	-9.0	20.0	28.4	39.2	-12.8	6.6	40.8	51.4	30.2
Loans Received	1.0	2.0	6.6	11.3	0.3	1.6	10.1	48.1	61.5
Loans Paid	—	—	-0.3	-0.1	-1.3	-1.1	-0.9	-0.6	-2.4
E. Short Term Private Capital	13.7	10.9	-11.7	0.3	0.6	0.2	43.3	7.9	6.3
Import Credit	16.3	10.2	3.0	3.8	3.7	13.5	17.8	13.3	6.3
Commercial Banks Net Foreign Assets	-6.5	5.1	1.4	0.4	-1.7	-4.0	0.9	-6.8	-1.2
Others	3.9	-4.4	-16.1	-3.9	-1.4	-9.3	24.6	1.4	1.2
F. Official Capital	-1.2	-1.2	1.8	13.0	-0.7	54.6	7.4	8.5	8.1
Long Term Loans Received	—	0.8	3.7	15.2	1.5	60.3	27.4	27.6	24.0
Long Term Loans Paid	-1.3	-1.9	-2.0	-2.1	-2.3	-8.9	-17.9	-19.9	-19.0
Others	0.1	-0.1	0.1	-0.1	0.1	3.2	-2.1	0.8	3.1
G. Net Errors & Omissions	-19.7	-28.3	16.9	-5.4	30.7	15.5	12.9	-5.6	6.2
H. Total (A through G)	2.3	6.5	-1.6	-6.3	6.6	-3.7	14.9	-33.6	-13.4
I. Central Reserve Bank Net Foreign Assets	-2.3	-6.5	1.6	6.3	-6.6	3.7	-14.9	33.6	13.4
IMF Account	—	—	-3.1	—	—	—	—	—	—
Foreign Assets (Increase)	-2.3	-6.5	4.7	6.3	-6.6	3.7	-14.9	33.6	2.4
Foreign Liabilities	—	—	—	—	—	—	—	—	11.0

Table Pr.–9 *(continued)*

	1959	1960	1961	1962	1963	1964	1965	1966
						(millions of dollars)		
A. Goods & Services	−45.9	−1.8	−35.2	−54.4	−99.7	−1.3	−88.8	−240.7
Exports F.O.B.	322.6	444.3	510.1	556.0	555.1	684.6	684.6	788.5
Imports F.O.B.	280.5	341.0	428.6	478.4	517.9	517.7	659.7	811.2
Balance of Trade	42.1	103.3	81.5	77.6	37.2	166.9	24.9	−22.7
Freight & Insurance on Goods	−39.6	−45.7	−53.3	−63.0	−62.5	−74.9	−83.3	−85.7
Investment Income	−43.8	−54.9	−62.6	−66.1	−72.0	−70.3	−82.0	−112.7
Other Services	−4.6	−4.5	−0.8	−2.9	−2.4	−20.4	−22.0	−19.6
Exports of Goods & Services	367.8	494.1	572.3	622.6	630.0	767.9	776.1	906.8
Imports of Goods & Services	409.7	491.9	603.1	672.3	723.6	759.7	920.7	1138.0
B. Transfer Payments	9.9	20.6	26.8	18.2	19.0	14.8	24.1	27.7
C. Balance on Current Account (A + B)	−36.0	18.8	−8.4	−36.2	−80.7	16.1	−138.3	−213.0
D. Long Term Private Capital	48.9	16.1	4.1	18.1	3.7	11.2	48.8	2.3
Direct Foreign Investment	18.2	11.1	14.2	16.4	−4.9	10.5	31.5	7.8
Loans Received	34.8	16.5	20.6	26.8	32.6	24.3	43.8	6.4
Loans Paid	−4.1	−11.5	−30.7	−25.1	−24.0	−23.6	−26.5	−11.9
E. Short Term Private Capital	3.0	4.9	15.3	22.7	−11.7	−44.7	−3.9	−9.9
Import Credit	5.6	0.3	22.7	33.9	24.8	−3.4	12.1	37.6
Commercial Banks Net Foreign Assets	−5.6	4.0	−0.6	−6.5	−16.1	−23.0	−7.4	−38.1
Others	3.0	0.6	−6.8	−4.7	−20.4	−18.3	−8.6	−9.4
F. Official Capital	−6.6	−9.3	−8.1	21.8	53.5	71.8	123.8	186.9
Long Term Loans Received	16.1	12.8	25.0	51.2	77.2	89.0	98.0	244.1
Long Term Loans Paid	−19.5	−24.3	−28.9	−31.4	−29.8	−30.0	−22.4	−66.5
Others	−3.2	2.2	−4.2	2.0	6.1	12.8	48.2	9.3
G. Net Errors & Omissions	8.1	2.2	31.4	−20.2	53.7	−29.4	−15.7	9.5
H. Total (A through G)	17.4	32.7	34.3	6.2	18.5	25.0	14.7	−24.2
I. Central Reserve Bank Net Foreign Assets	−17.4	−32.7	−34.3	−6.2	−18.5	−25.0	−14.7	24.2
IMF Account	−0.6	−0.6	−0.6	−0.6	−0.6			−2.4
Foreign Assets (Increase)	−21.3	−16.6	−33.7	−5.6	−17.9	−25.0	−14.7	24.6
Foreign Liabilities	4.5	−15.5						2.0

Source: Banco Central de Reserva del Peru, *Cuentas Nacionales del Peru, 1950–67* (1968) p. 40.

Table Pr.-10 Government Receipts and Expenditures, 1950–1966

	1950	1951	1952	1953	1954	1955	1956	1957	1958
					(millions of soles)				
Receipts	2,044	2,526	3,805	3,096	3,504	3,901	4,581	5,027	5,026
Profit Tax	903	1,039	1,010	842	1,046	1,098	1,220	1,331	1,281
Receipts from Individuals	206	245	285	336	413	469	521	575	724
Direct Taxes	117	125	152	184	194	222	233	263	340
Contributions to Social Security	45	71	80	85	151	168	196	218	264
Non-Tax Payments	44	49	53	67	68	79	92	94	120
Indirect Taxes	695	1,095	1,357	1,791	1,854	2,106	2,558	2,821	2,706
Import Duties	254	583	648	746	767	806	1,006	1,127	1,022
Others	441	512	709	1,045	1,087	1,300	1,552	1,694	1,684
Non-Tax Payments of Businesses	240	147	153	127	191	228	282	300	315
Expenditures	1,737	2,220	2,691	3,120	3,181	4,133	4,986	5,332	5,789
Consumption Expenditures	1,132	1,606	1,682	1,982	2,071	2,240	2,958	3,127	3,504
Wages & Salaries	953	1,316	1,418	1,535	1,633	1,772	2,233	2,382	2,780
Others	179	290	264	447	438	468	725	745	724
Subsidies	205	122	174	318	338	404	568	647	601
Transfer Payments to Individuals	167	218	250	271	280	423	500	679	631
Transfer Payments Abroad	18	19	23	18	15	21	22	22	23
Interest on the Public Debt	38	38	43	46	66	91	113	119	132
Current Expenditure	1,560	2,003	2,172	2,635	2,770	3,179	4,161	4,594	4,891
Machinery & Equipment	15	15	31	23	51	142	31	43	44
New Construction	162	202	488	462	360	812	794	695	854
Investment Expenditures	177	217	519	485	411	954	825	738	898
Saving on Current Account	484	523	633	461	734	722	420	433	135

Table Pr.–10 (continued)

	1959	1960	1961	1962	1963	1964	1965	1966
				(millions of soles)				
Receipts	6,438	8,532	10,102	11,439	13,694	16,507	20,478	24,261
Profit Tax	1,546	2,375	2,588	2,778	3,196	3,296	3,457	3,583
Receipts from Individuals	1,027	1,205	1,330	1,590	2,234	2,412	3,709	4,883
Direct Taxes	388	491	543	679	689	625	1,035	1,659
Contributions to Social Security	486	550	597	735	1,307	1,551	2,304	2,773
Non-Tax Payments	153	164	190	176	238	236	370	451
Indirect Taxes	3,476	4,523	5,614	6,278	7,498	9,986	12,177	14,448
Import Duties	1,259	1,601	1,965	2,058	2,345	3,619	5,053	5,702
Others	2,217	2,922	3,649	4,220	5,153	6,367	7,124	8,746
Non-Tax Payments of Businesses	389	429	570	793	766	813	1,135	1,347
Expenditures	6,753	7,680	9,773	11,557	13,863	18,436	23,933	29,003
Consumption Expenditures	4,199	4,776	5,938	6,771	7,714	10,213	12,542	14,796
Wages & Salaries	3,499	3,898	4,796	5,563	6,562	8,521	10,569	12,715
Others	700	878	1,142	1,208	1,152	1,692	1,973	2,081
Subsidies	682	882	1,151	1,523	1,735	2,158	2,493	2,380
Transfer Payments to Individuals	952	1,141	1,246	1,535	3,188	4,025	5,247	6,931
Transfer Payments Abroad	35	41	30	21	30	48	29	21
Interest on the Public Debt	196	181	180	162	203	217	575	625
Current Expenditure	6,064	7,021	8,545	10,012	12,870	16,661	20,886	24,753
Machinery & Equipment	36	42	121	156	126	303	405	538
New Construction	653	617	1,107	1,389	867	1,472	2,642	3,712
Investment Expenditures	689	659	1,228	1,545	993	1,775	3,047	4,250
Saving on Current Account	374	1,511	1,557	1,427	824	−154	−408	−492

Source: Banco Central de Reserva del Peru, *Cuentas Nacionales del Peru*, 1950–67 (1968), 1950–65 (1966), Table 12.

Suggested Readings on Peru

The student is expected to be familiar with starred (*) items.

1. Thorbecke, Erik, and Condos, Apostolos. "Macroeconomic Growth and Development Models of the Peruvian Economy." Edited by I. Adelman and E. Thorbecke. *Theory and Design of Economic Development.* Johns Hopkins Press, 1966, pp. 181–208.

2. Goldberger, A. J. "Comment." Ibid., pp. 208–209.

3. *Thorp, Rosemary. "Inflation and Orthodox Economic Policy in Peru." *Bulletin of the Oxford University Institute of Statistics,* vol. 29, Aug. 1967, pp. 185–210.

4. *Hunt, Shane J. "Distribution, Growth and Government Economic Behaviour in Peru." Woodrow Wilson School Development Research Project Discussion Paper No. 7. (To be published in 1971 in *Government and Economic Development,* edited by Gustav Ranis, Yale University Press.)

5. Schydlowsky, Daniel M. "Distribution, Growth, and Government Economic Behavior in Peru; Comment." Harvard University, Center for International Affairs. Economic Development Report No. 133. (To be published in 1971 in *Government and Economic Development,* edited by Gustav Ranis, Yale University Press.)

Case 8: Monetary Policy

In January of each year, the Peruvian Central Reserve Bank prepares a monetary program for the year. This program focuses on three main variables: primary credit creation by the Central Bank; deficit finance to the Government; and credit expansion to the private sector. In addition to serving as a policy guide for the year, this program is the basis for the yearly consultations with the IMF under Article VIII and often gets written as a target into a Stand-By Agreement.

In January 1967 you are called in to participate in the preparation of the monetary program for the year. As he opens the meeting, the General Manager of the Bank points out that the performance of the economy in 1966 was not fully satisfactory in some respects. The real growth rate achieved was 5.7 per cent, which compared favorably to the 5 per cent of 1965 but much less well to the 8 per cent attained in 1964. Prices, as measured by the cost of living index, increased by 8.9 per cent which is a considerable improvement over the 11.5 per cent of 1965, and better than the 9.5 per cent of 1964, yet is still very high, especially in view of the fiscal situation.

Credit to the government expanded by 50 per cent in 1966, after having increased by over 80 per cent in 1965 and over 40 per cent in 1964.

The cumulative effect of this credit expansion is believed to have contributed substantially to the increase in prices. Credit restraint on lending to the private sector was not able to counteract this fully despite a tough reserve requirement policy. From January 1 to May 26, Commercial Banks were required to maintain the following reserves:

1. On all liabilities in domestic currency:
   a) 30 per cent on the total; plus
   b) 40 per cent on the increase since June 25, 1965; plus
   c) 30 per cent on the increase since Nov. 30, 1965.

2. On all liabilities in foreign currency:
   a) 30 per cent on the total; plus
   b) 40 per cent on the increase since May 31, 1965; plus
   c) 30 per cent on the increase since Nov. 30, 1965.

From May 27 to December 31, 1966, the requirement was as follows:

1. On all liabilities in domestic currency:
   a) 29 per cent on the total; plus
   b) 40 per cent on the increase since June 25, 1965.

2. On all liabilities in foreign currency:
   a) 30 per cent on the total; plus
   b) 40 per cent on the increase since May 31, 1965; plus
   c) 30 per cent on the increase since November 30, 1965.

These regulations imply reserve requirements of 100 per cent on all increases in liabilities during the period January to May, and 69 per cent and

100 per cent on increase in domestic and foreign currency liabilities, respectively, during the period June to December. As a result, expansion of credit on private account was only 15 per cent in 1966, a reduction from the 25 per cent of 1965. Furthermore, the private share of total new credit fell to 55 per cent from 67 per cent in 1965 and of this 55 per cent, one-half was channeled through the (production) Development Banks. The net result of the monetary developments was a disheartening increase of 22 per cent in the money supply, only slightly less than the 28 per cent of 1965.

The balance of payments has begun to reflect the internal inflation, making 1966 the first year without a surplus since 1958. The deficit of $24.6 million has reduced reserves to $153 million or the equivalent of about 1.6 months of imports.

The 1967 program will concentrate on the twin objectives of price stabilization and balance of payments equilibrium. A price increase of not more than five per cent should be aimed at; the loss of reserves should be kept to a maximum of $10 million. On the other hand, growth should not slow down below five per cent.

In outlining the targets, the General Manager notes that the Finance Ministry has prepared a pro-forma budget showing a deficit of about 4000 million soles with approximately half to be financed from foreign loans (Table 8–1). The Monetary Committee should review this forecast and assess its realism. Furthermore, the Committee should prepare its own estimate of the balance of payments for 1967 and use the result in its work.

Among the considerations the Committee should bear in mind are the following:

1. An excessive tightening of credit in the private sector may well have repercussions on the level of output and growth. Therefore, preemption on the part of the exchequer of a high proportion of new credit may endanger the attainment of the output goal and at the same time generate demand pressures and cause increases in prices and imports. On the other hand, excess liquidity for the private sector will only serve to expand demand for imports and decrease the foreign exchange reserves.

2. The private sector has access to foreign credit lines which it is likely to use if it is short of funds and does not see too large an exchange risk. Tight domestic credit may thus improve the balance of payments on capital account. At the same time, however, a large fiscal deficit is likely to undermine confidence in the economic policy and the exchange rate and will lead to reduced foreign borrowing and, quite possibly, to the outright export of capital. Such a development would reduce domestic private liquidity and have negative output effects which would feed into higher prices and greater imports thus compounding the problem.

3. The banking system is in a substantial profit squeeze resulting from the high reserve requirements. It is therefore worth considering whether to accommodate part of the government's financing needs through loans from the Commercial Banks with offsetting reserve requirement reductions.

In short, the Committee's report should answer the following questions:

1. Are the targets consistent and attainable? If not, what combinations of targets do you feel can be attained?

2. How much should the primary credit expansion of the Central Bank be in 1967?

3. How should it be distributed between the Government and the private sector?

4. What should the reserve requirement policy be?

The General Manager wishes to see the Committee's recommendations backed by the following forecasts:

1. Government Budget (revised)
2. Balance of Payments
3. Monetary Accounts:
   a) Consolidated balance sheet of the banking system.
   b) Breakdown between Central Bank and rest of system.

Table 8–1   *Pro-forma Budget for 1967 (Millions of soles)*

A.	Receipts	28,000	
	Profit Tax		4,200
	Receipts from Individuals		5,700
	Direct Taxes		2,000
	Contributions to Social Security		3,300
	Non-tax Payments		400
	Indirect Taxes		16,600
	Import Duties		6,600
	Others		10,000
	Non-tax Payments		1,500
B.	Expenditures	32,000	
	Consumption Expenditures		16,500
	Wages & Salaries		14,100
	Others		2,400
	Subsidies		2,600
	Transfer Payments to Individuals		7,600
	Transfer Payments Abroad		25
	Interest on the Public Debt		775
	Total Current Expenditure		27,500
	Machinery and Equipment		600
	New Construction		3,900
	Total Investment Expenditure		4,500
C.	Deficit	4,000	
D.	Foreign Loan Disbursements — US $80 million = soles 2,150 million		

Table 8-2A Peru: Monetary Statistics 1959–1966, Consolidated Balance Sheet of The Banking System (Millions of soles)

	Dec. 1959	Dec. 1960	Dec. 1961	Dec. 1962	Dec. 1963	Dec. 1964	Dec. 1965	Dec. 1966
A. *Net Foreign Assets*								
1. Gold	1,592.0	1,916.3	2,841.1	3,667.5	4,514.1	5,449.8	4,745.8	5,036.3
2. Gold Subscription to IMF	434.9	837.5	1,011.0	1,611.2	1,868.7	2,206.1	2,594.8	2,636.0
3. Other assets in foreign currency	190.5	201.0	271.8	234.7	251.4	251.4	251.4	315.1
4. Liabilities in foreign currency	1,053.9	1,081.2	1,924.2	2,202.1	2,805.7	3,591.1	3,941.2	4,221.9
	−87.3	−203.4	−311.9	−380.5	−411.7	−598.8	−2,041.6	−2,136.7
C. *Domestic Credit*	9,293.6	10,764.9	11,960.2	12,873.4	14,486.0	17,535.0	23,539.2	28,617.2
1. To the Public Sector (Net)	3,223.7	2,913.3	2,369.9	2,111.8	2,034.5	2,804.7	5,112.1	7,605.2
a. Credit and Investment	4,337.6	4,458.8	4,480.8	4,221.4	4,957.0	6,597.0	10,630.1	12,976.5
to the Central Government	3,947.8	4,028.9	4,005.9	3,678.7	4,248.9	5,630.9	9,346.0	11,287.7
to the Independent Public Sub-Sector	341.7	375.4	411.2	445.8	611.0	856.7	1,140.9	1,514.6
to Local Governments	48.1	54.2	63.7	96.9	98.0	109.4	143.2	174.2
b. Less: Deposits	−1,113.9	−1,545.2	−2,110.9	−2,109.6	−2,923.4	−3,792.3	−5,518.0	−6,371.3
of the Central Government	−844.9	−1,010.9	−1,361.5	−1,208.0	−1,852.0	−1,695.7	−3,297.7	−2,638.7
of the Independent Public Sub-Sector	−245.7	−498.9	−714.2	−862.2	−1,034.3	−1,999.9	−2,015.2	−2,532.6
of the Local Governments	−23.3	−35.4	−35.2	−39.4	−37.1	−96.7	−205.1	−200.0
2. To the Private Sector	7,365.5	8,784.7	10,532.4	12,235.7	14,044.7	16,491.0	20,732.0	23,855.6
3. Other Net Assets[1]	−1,295.6	−933.1	−942.1	−1,474.1	−1,593.2	−1,760.7	−2,304.9	−2,843.6
Assets = Liabilities	10,885.6	12,681.2	14,801.3	16,540.9	19,000.1	22,984.8	28,285.0	33,653.5
D. *Liabilities to Foreign Institutions* (Long Term)	—	177.0	180.3	163.0	202.0	250.9	427.0	629.2
F. *Liabilities to the Private Sector*	10,885.6	12,504.2	14,621.0	16,377.9	18,798.1	22,733.9	27,858.0	33,024.3
1. Monetary Stock	5,742.9	6,519.6	7,600.7	8,035.6	9,209.9	11,158.0	13,050.1	15,943.3
Notes and Coins	2,827.8	3,074.9	3,445.4	3,995.0	4,721.1	5,840.7	6,886.3	7,770.1
Demand Deposits	2,915.1	3,444.7	4,155.3	4,040.6	4,488.8	5,317.3	6,163.8	8,173.2
2. Quasi-Money	4,012.6	4,729.1	5,549.2	6,661.1	7,841.8	9,669.7	12,360.3	13,726.8
Time Deposits	1,278.7	1,771.9	1,985.7	2,317.6	2,471.1	2,902.2	3,994.3	3,372.9
Savings Deposits	1,711.5	2,018.1	2,386.8	2,874.4	3,483.9	4,255.7	5,419.8	6,545.9
Deposits in foreign currency	1,022.4	939.1	1,176.7	1,469.1	1,886.8	2,511.8	2,946.2	3,808.0
3. Other Liabilities[2]	1,130.1	1,255.5	1,471.1	1,681.2	1,746.4	1,906.2	2,447.6	3,354.2

Source: Banco Central de Reserva del Peru, *Cuentas Monetarias*, Serie 12, Lima, Marzo 1968.
[1] Includes mainly government equity, checks in process of collection (float), fixed assets.
[2] Includes mainly equity owned by the private sector, bonds and retained earnings.

Table 8–2B Peru: Monetary Statistics 1959–1966, Central Reserve Bank (Millions of soles)

	Dec. 1959	1960	1961	1962	1963	1964	1965	1966
A. *Net Foreign Assets*	1,131.5	1,547.6	2,470.3	3,133.3	3,632.7	4,304.3	4,698.4	4,101.8
1. Gold	266.9	643.9	778.2	1,270.4	1,538.6	1,806.8	1,801.1	1,737.4
2. Gold Subscription to IMF	190.5	201.0	217.8	234.7	251.4	251.4	251.4	315.1
3. Other assets in foreign currency	674.1	702.7	1,474.3	1,628.2	1,842.7	2,246.1	2,645.9	2,103.9
4. Liabilities in foreign currency								−54.6
C. *Domestic Credit*	3,501.9	3,832.9	3,925.4	3,978.4	4,386.9	5,723.1	6,637.1	8,098.8
1. To the Public Sector (Net)	2,922.9	3,045.8	3,140.4	2,679.2	3,292.8	4,394.8	4,500.3	6,567.0
a. Credit and Investment to the Central Government	3,235.7	3,191.0	3,218.3	2,773.7	3,507.0	4,558.2	4,543.5	6,607.6
to the Independent Public Sub-Sector	3,235.7	3,191.0	3,218.3	2,773.7	3,507.0	4,558.2	4,543.5	6,607.6
b. Less Deposits	−312.8	−145.2	−77.9	−94.5	−214.7	−163.4	−43.2	−40.6
of the Central Government	−303.7	−145.1	−70.2	−91.8	−206.1	−153.5	−26.8	−36.2
of the Independent Public Sub-Sector of the Local Governments	−9.1	−0.1	−7.7	−2.7	−8.6	−9.9	−16.4	−4.4
3. To the Banks	1,151.2	906.7	873.0	1,380.1	1,262.6	1,349.1	2,117.8	1,471.8
4. Other Net Assets[1]	−572.2	−119.6	−88.0	−80.9	−168.5	−20.8	19.0	60.0
Assets = Liabilities	4,633.4	5,380.5	6,395.7	7,111.7	8,019.6	10,027.4	11,335.5	12,200.6
E. *Liabilities to Banks*	1,678.1	2,262.8	2,900.9	3,094.5	3,269.1	4,108.3	4,385.2	4,359.3
1. Specialized Banks	57.1	139.8	186.8	77.6	281.4	173.8	310.0	142.2
Notes and Coins	39.2	36.5	62.7	37.9	78.7	87.1	152.4	121.5
Deposits	17.9	103.3	124.1	39.7	202.7	86.7	157.6	20.7
2. Commercial Banks	1,618.0	2,118.5	2,703.2	3,013.5	2,986.3	3,856.2	4,049.5	4,132.4
Notes and Coins	532.0	611.9	816.8	943.8	1,082.9	1,206.6	1,395.6	1,467.0
Deposits	1,086.0	1,506.6	1,886.4	2,069.7	1,903.4	2,649.6	2,653.9	2,665.4
Foreign Exchange Certificates								
3. State Bank	3.0	4.5	10.9	3.4	1.4	78.3	25.7	84.7
Notes and Coins	3.0	4.5	10.9	3.4	1.4	51.4	5.6	9.6
Deposits						26.9	20.1	75.1
F. *Liabilities to Private Sector*	2,955.3	3,117.7	3,494.8	4,017.2	4,750.5	5,919.1	6,950.3	7,841.3
Notes and Coins	2,827.8	3,074.9	3,445.4	3,995.0	4,721.1	5,840.7	6,886.3	7,791.7
a. Issued	3,402.0	3,727.8	4,335.8	4,980.1	5,884.1	7,185.8	8,439.9	9,389.8
b. Less: in Banks	574.2	652.9	890.4	985.1	1,163.0	1,343.1	1,553.6	1,598.1
Demand Deposits	8.2	9.6	15.4	21.0	28.2	73.7	62.9	49.1
Foreign Exchange Deposits	90.2	3.3	2.9	1.2	1.2	4.7	1.1	0.5
Capital and Reserves	29.1	29.9	31.3					

Source: Banco Central de Reserva del Perú, *Cuentas Monetarias*, Serie 12, Lima, Marzo 1968.

Table 8-2C Peru: Monetary Statistics 1959–1966, Consolidated Balance Sheet of the Commercial State and Development Banks (Millions of soles)

	Dec. 1959	Dec. 1960	Dec. 1961	Dec. 1962	Dec. 1963	Dec. 1964	Dec. 1965	Dec. 1966
A. *Net Foreign Assets*	460.5	368.7	370.8	534.2	881.4	1,145.5	47.4	934.5
1. Gold	168.0	193.6	232.8	340.8	330.1	399.3	793.7	898.6
3. Other assets in foreign currency	379.8	379.0	449.9	573.9	963.0	1,345.0	1,295.3	2,118.0
4. Liabilities in foreign currency	−87.3	−203.9	−311.9	−380.5	−411.7	−598.8	−2,041.6	−2,082.1
B. *Cash and Deposits in the Central Reserve Bank*	1,773.7	2,253.1	2,894.2	3,283.5	3,280.0	4,279.0	4,387.4	4,422.6
1. Cash	574.2	652.9	876.4	985.1	1,163.1	1,345.1	1,553.6	1,619.7
2. Deposits	1,199.5	1,600.2	2,017.8	2,298.4	2,116.9	2,933.9	2,833.8	2,802.9
C. *Domestic Credit*	6,847.3	7,671.4	8,734.2	9,923.1	11,148.8	12,739.4	18,590.7	21,319.3
1. To the Public Sector (Net)	300.8	−132.5	−770.5	−567.4	−1,258.3	−1,590.1	611.8	1,038.2
a. Credit and Investment	1,101.9	1,267.5	1,262.5	1,447.7	1,450.9	2,038.8	6,086.6	6,368.9
to the Central Government	712.1	837.3	787.1	905.0	741.9	1,072.7	4,802.5	4,680.1
to the Independent Sub-Sector	341.7	376.0	410.8	445.8	611.0	856.7	1,140.9	1,514.6
to the Local Governments	48.1	54.3	64.6	96.9	98.0	109.4	143.2	174.2
b. Less: Deposits	−801.1	−1,400.0	−2,033.0	−2,015.1	−2,709.2	−3,628.9	−5,474.8	−5,330.7
of the Central Government	−541.2	−865.8	−1,291.3	−1,116.2	−1,645.9	−1,542.2	−3,270.9	−2,602.5
of the Independent Sub-Sector	−236.6	−498.8	−706.5	−859.5	−1,026.2	−1,990.0	−1,998.8	−2,528.2
of the Local Governments	−23.3	−35.4	−35.2	−39.4	−37.1	−96.7	−205.1	−200.0
2. To the Private Sector	7,365.5	8,784.7	10,532.4	12,235.7	14,044.7	16,491.0	20,732.0	23,855.6
3. Other Net Assets[1]	−819.0	−980.0	−1,027.7	−1,745.2	−1,637.6	−2,161.5	−2,753.1	−3,574.5
Assets = Liabilities	9,081.5	10,293.2	11,999.2	13,740.8	15,310.2	18,163.9	23,025.5	26,676.4
E. *Liabilities to the Central Reserve Bank*	1,151.2	906.7	873.0	1,380.1	1,262.6	1,349.1	2,117.8	1,471.8
F. *Liabilities to the Private Sector*	7,930.0	9,386.5	11,126.2	12,360.7	14,047.6	16,814.8	20,907.7	25,204.6
1. Demand Deposits	2,906.9	3,435.1	4,139.9	4,019.6	4,460.6	5,243.6	6,100.9	8,124.1
2. Time Deposits	1,278.7	1,771.9	1,985.7	2,317.6	2,471.1	2,902.2	3,944.3	3,372.9
3. Savings Deposits	1,708.5	2,018.1	2,386.8	2,874.4	3,483.9	4,255.7	5,419.8	6,545.9
4. Foreign Exchange Deposits	932.2	935.8	1,173.8	1,467.9	1,885.6	2,507.1	2,945.1	3,807.5
5. Other Liabilities[2]	1,104.0	1,225.6	1,440.0	1,681.2	1,746.4	1,906.2	2,447.6	3,354.2

Source: Banco Central de Reserva del Peru, *Cuentas Monetarias*, Serie 12, Lima, Marzo 1968.
[1] Includes mainly government equity, checks in process of collection (float), fixed assets.
[2] Includes mainly equity owned by the private sector, bonds and retained earnings.
Note: Liabilities subject to reserve requirements: 1) Demand deposits, 2) Time deposits, 3) Savings deposits, 4) Foreign exchange deposits, 5) Liabilities in foreign currency. Reserves: 1) Gold, 2) Other assets in foreign currency, 3) Cash and deposits in Central Reserve Bank.

Case 9: Fiscal Policy

The first draft of the 1967 budget had shown a deficit of 6,000 million soles; the second draft had reduced this figure to 4,000 million. Of this total, perhaps 1,500 to 2,000 million were financable from foreign project loans. The Finance Minister's advisers assured him if the budget were executed in this form, the balance of payments situation in 1967 would deteriorate and prices increase at rates substantially above the acceptable five per cent. A crisis of confidence might ensue, causing capital flight, an unsustainable loss of reserves and eventually either devaluation or exchange control. Their advice, therefore, is to substantially reduce and, if possible, eliminate the deficit.

As the budget was reexamined once more, two schools of thought could be detected. The fiscal conservatives advised that the budget be balanced by cutting expenditures. They marshalled a number of arguments in support of their position:

1. The role of government had expanded greatly since 1960 with expenditures going from 10.8 per cent of GNP to 17 per cent in that period (see Table 9–1).

2. Government consumption expenditure was bloated; not only had it tripled since 1960; it was high even by Latin American standards (see Tables 9–1, 9–2).

3. Government investment had also increased substantially since 1960. In absolute terms, it had grown by more than six fold. In relative terms it had grown to absorb 35 per cent of government expenditure by 1966 which compares very favorably to 20.6 per cent in 1960. If the government enterprises are excluded, the share of investment had risen from 12 per cent to 22 per cent (see Table 9–4).

4. The revenue system had been performing satisfactorily showing an ex post income elasticity greater than one. It was best, therefore, not to tamper with it.

5. Any new revenue, to be of a meaningful magnitude would have to come from increased import duties or turn-over taxes. Such an increase was undesirable on grounds of equity, price stability, efficiency and incentive and should be avoided at all costs.

The liberals suggested that expenditures should be held down as much as possible but that an increase in revenue was essential. They supported their position with the following arguments.

1. A cut in consumption expenditures would require firing government employees which would have very undesirable social and political effects.

2. A cut in investment expenditures would reduce the growth rate and in addition imperil the balance of payments through the loss of project aid tied to local component provisions (see Table 9–9).

3. Although the share of government revenue in GNP had increased, the share of expenditure in GNP increased even faster. An excess of 2 percentage points of revenue over expenditure in 1960 had turned to a shortfall of 3.5 percentage points (see Table 9–5).

4. The share of consumption expenditure (which includes such items as education and health) in total government expenditure had been held down over the years. Since 1960 it had declined from 80 per cent to 65 per cent. (See Table 9–4.)

5. International comparisons showed Peru as having the seventh lowest ratio of government consumption to GNP and the fifth lowest per capita expenditure on government consumption for the 19 Latin American republics (see Table 9–3).

6. The revenue system had shown only a satisfactory performance because it had been continuously "tampered" with, particularly by means of repeated increases in import and turn-over taxes.

The Finance Minister wishes to know:

1. Should he cut expenditures or raise taxes or both.

2. What would constitute a reasonable tax package yielding 1,500 to 2,000 million soles of new revenue in 1967 with as little administrative reorganization as possible. He would like to see more than one alternative policy package and wishes to have each of them discussed from the following points of view:
   a. rate and yield
   b. equity (progressivity)
   c. inflationary impact
   d. balance of payments effects
   e. contribution to elasticity of system
   f. effects on the allocation of resources
   g. effects on economic growth.

Table 9–1   *Peru: The Size of Government Operations (Millions of current soles)*

	Expenditure on Consumption (1)	Investment		Total Expenditure (4) = 1 + 2 + 3	GNP (5)
		Central Gov. (2)	Indep. Enterprise (3)		
1960	4,776	659	583	6,018	55,518
1961	5,938	1,228	1,640	8,806	62,294
1962	6,771	1,545	1,254	9,570	71,700
1963	7,714	993	2,100	10,807	78,710
1964	10,213	1,775	2,805	14,793	78,710
1965	12,542	3,047	3,131	18,720	113,000
1966	14,796	4,250	3,732	22,778	134,016

Table 9–1 (continued)

	Gov. Expenditure	Ratios Central Gov.	Central Gov.
	GNP 4/5	GNP (1 + 2)/5	Total Gov. (1 + 2)/4
1960	.108	.098	.903
1961	.141	.115	.814
1962	.133	.116	.869
1963	.137	.111	.806
1964	.156	.126	.810
1965	.166	.138	.833
1966	.170	.142	.836

Source: Banco Central de Reserva del Peru, *Cuentas Nacionales del Peru* (1968)

Table 9–2 *Latin America: The Importance of Government Consumption Expenditure (1960 Dollars at Purchasing Power Parity Conversion)*

Country	Government Consumption (millions)	GDP	Ratio	Country	Per Capita Gov. Consumption
Ecuador	368	1,512	.243	Argentina	194
Dominican Rep.	204	863	.236	Uruguay	182
Costa Rica	137	660	.208	Chile	136
Brazil	4,949	24,080	.206	Venezuela	116
Panama	108	536	.201	Costa Rica	114
Honduras	87	448	.194	Panama	105
Bolivia	143	737	.194	Ecuador	85
PERU	725	3,899	.186	PERU	72
Argentina	4,001	21,851	.183	Brazil	70
Uruguay	453	2,522	.180	Dominican Rep.	67
Chile	1,062	6,304	.168	El Salvador	51
El Salvador	128	765	.167	Colombia	46
Paraguay	78	524	.149	Guatemala	45
Haiti	63	436	.144	Honduras	45
Guatemala	169	1,230	.137	Paraguay	44
Venezuela	854	6,388	.134	Mexico	41
Nicaragua	54	409	.132	Bolivia	37
Colombia	704	6,133	.115	Nicaragua	37
Mexico	1,467	20,965	.070	Haiti	15

Source: S. N. Braithwaite, "The Measurement of Latin American Real Income in U.S. Dollars," *Economic Bulletin for Latin America*, vol. 12, no. 2, October 1967, pp. 107–142.

Table 9–3 Latin America: The Importance of Government Consumption Expenditure (1960 Dollars at Exchange Rate Conversion)

Country	Government Consumption (millions)	GDP	Ratio	Country	Per Capita Gov. Consumption
Brazil	2,693	17,575	.153	Venezuela	144
Venezuela	1,058	7,648	.138	Chile	62
Ecuador	120	928	.129	Argentina	52
Dominican Rep.	92	723	.127	Panama	49
Costa Rica	55	463	.119	Costa Rica	45
Panama	50	420	.119	Uruguay	43
Chile	485	4,724	.103	Brazil	38
El Salvador	57	567	.101	Dominican Rep.	30
Honduras	26	298	.098	Ecuador	28
Argentina	1,066	11,802	.090	El Salvador	23
Uruguay	107	1,188	.090	Guatemala	21
Haiti	26	298	.087	Honduras	19
PERU	174	2,074	.084	Nicaragua	19
Nicaragua	28	337	.083	Mexico	18
Bolivia	30	376	.080	PERU	17
Paraguay	22	283	.078	Colombia	16
Guatemala	80	1,021	.078	Paraguay	12
Colombia	251	4,003	.063	Bolivia	8
Mexico	639	12,471	.051	Haiti	6

Source: S. N. Braithwaite, "The Measurement of Latin American Real Income in U.S. Dollars," *Economic Bulletin for Latin America*, vol. 12, no. 2, October 1967, pp. 107–142.

Table 9–4 Peru: The Distribution of Government Expenditure

	Total Gov. Investment / Total Gov. Expenditure	Central Gov. Investment / Central Gov. Exp.	Central Gov. Investment / Total Gov. I.
1960	.206	.121	.531
1961	.326	.171	.428
1962	.292	.186	.552
1963	.286	.114	.321
1964	.310	.148	.388
1965	.330	.195	.493
1966	.350	.223	.532

Source: Banco Central de Reserva del Peru, *Cuentas Nacionales del Peru 1950–67*, Lima, 1968.

Table **9–5** *Peru: Level of Government Revenue* and Expenditure*

Year	Revenue	Expenditure	GNP	Ratio	
				Rev.	Exp.
1960	8,532	7,680	55,518	.154	.138
1961	10,102	9,773	62,294	.162	.157
1962	11,439	11,557	71,700	.160	.161
1963	13,694	13,863	78,710	.174	.176
1964	16,507	18,436	94,994	.174	.194
1965	20,478	23,933	113,000	.181	.212
1966	24,261	29,003	134,016	.181	.216

Source: Banco Central de Reserva del Peru, *Cuentas Nacionales del Peru*, 1950–67, Lima, 1968.
* Includes Central and Local Governments; does not include independent enterprises.

Table **9–6** *Percentage Distribution of Government Expenditure*

	General administration	Armed Forces	Justice and Police	Education	Health	Development	Transfers[1]	Other
1900	28.5%	25.1%	22.2%	2.9%	0.7%	2.0%	9.6%	9.0%
1905	23.8	35.6	14.3	4.5	2.9	3.3	13.9	1.7
1910	12.5	52.9	11.3	8.1	1.2	2.1	9.4	2.4
1915	18.6	27.4	17.7	10.1	0.7	1.7	16.3	7.4
1920	21.5	23.4	14.6	10.6	5.9	11.0	11.3	1.7
1929	25.8	22.8	14.5	11.7	4.9	8.3	10.9	1.1
1942	19.4	24.7	15.5	10.5	6.4	11.8	11.0	0.6
1945	14.7	26.3	14.8	13.3	7.7	10.9	11.6	0.7
1950	13.3	24.6	15.2	16.0	5.2	14.5	10.6	0.5
1955	11.8	23.8	13.9	14.8	9.4	15.3	10.4	0.6
1960	11.4	21.6	12.1	20.6	8.3	12.1	13.3	0.7
1965	9.6	15.6	12.2	29.4	6.4	16.8	9.3	0.7

Source: Shane J. Hunt, "Distribution, Growth and Government Behavior in Peru," Woodrow Wilson School Development Research Project Discussion Paper No. 7, Table 5.
[1] Miscellaneous current and capital transfers to Development Banks, Social Security, and other independent public entities.

Table 9–7 *Growth of Government Revenue (Revenues expressed as per cent of current price GNP)*

	Total revenue	All Indirect taxes[1]	Taxes on imports	Excise taxes	Turnover tax	All Direct taxes[2]	Major taxes on income from	
							labor	capital
1942–45	11.2%			0.83%	0.17%			
1945–50	11.6			0.42	0.27		0.65%	4.3%
1950–55	12.7	6.3%	2.8%	0.30	0.23	5.8%	0.67	3.9
1955–60	13.3	7.4	2.9	0.35	0.46	5.3	0.73	3.0
1960–65	16.0	9.2	3.4	0.29	2.49	6.1	0.72	3.2

Revenue elasticities

1942–65	1.63**			−0.22**	5.05**			
1950–65	1.82**	2.54**	2.02**	0.86	8.70**	1.10	1.02	0.17*

Source: Shane J. Hunt, "Distribution, Growth and Government Behaviour in Peru," Woodrow Wilson School Development Research Project Discussion Paper No. 7, Table 7.
[1] Includes taxes on imports, excise taxes, turnover tax, tax on bank loans and surplus of state monopolies.
[2] Includes income taxes on persons and corporations, export taxes, social security contributions and fees for government services.
* Significantly different from unitary elasticity at 5% level.
** Significantly different from unitary elasticity at 1% level.

Table 9–8 *Percentage Distribution of Government Revenue*

	Export taxes	Profit taxes	Personal income taxes	Import taxes	Turnover taxes	Excise taxes and monopoly revenue	Other revenue[1]
1900	0 %	2.9%	0 %	59.5	1.6%	27.7%	8.3%
1905	0	3.6	0	50.9	1.4	35.1	8.9
1910	0	4.2	0	49.9	1.2	29.0	15.7
1915	0	5.5	0	28.5	1.4	39.1	25.5
1920	32.6	3.4	0	26.1	0.9	17.7	19.3
1929							
1942	16.0		15.0	11.1	1.5	15.9	40.6
1945	16.5	16.1	5.7	9.0	1.6	11.7	39.4
1950	27.5	13.9	5.4	13.0	2.4	7.0	30.7
1955	11.0	12.3	5.4	21.7	1.5	6.7	41.4
1960	8.9	15.6	5.5	19.6	1.5	5.8	36.2
1965	4.0	10.4	3.5	23.9	19.6	3.6	35.0

Source: Shane J. Hunt, "Distribution, Growth and Government Behaviour in Peru," Woodrow Wilson School Development Research Project Discussion Paper No. 7, Table 9.
[1] Includes payments for government services other than post office, public property income other than from public corporations, minor sales taxes, property and real estate profits tax, inheritance tax.

Table 9–9 Central Government Investment Tied to Project Aid 1966 and 1967 (Millions of soles)

	1966			Forecast 1967		
	Domestic Financing	Foreign Debt Utilization	Total	Domestic Financing	Foreign Debt Utilization[4]	Total
A. *Transport*	479.1	1,620.3	2,099.4	385.2	1,183.5	1,568.7
1. Roads	397.1	1,571.6	1,968.7	338.3	1.087.8	1,426.1
2. Railroads	23.2	—	23.2	9.8	—	9.8
3. Port works	58.8	48.7	107.5	37.1	95.7	132.8
B. *Agriculture*	251.4	317.9	569.3	54.5	369.0	423.5
1. Irrigation works	169.8	239.7	409.5	42.3	356.1	398.4
2. Agricultural Development[1]	81.6	78.2	159.8	12.2	12.9	25.1
C. *Social Development*	340.3	57.0	397.3	105.0	151.2	256.2
1. Sanitation	78.8	44.1	122.9	27.0	59.8	86.8
2. Public Works	38.0	—	38.0	6.4	—	6.4
3. School Buildings	128.0	—	128.0	66.8	—	66.8
4. Electrification	95.5	—	95.5	4.8	1.8	6.6
5. Community Development	—	12.9	12.9	—	89.6	89.6
D. *Others*	181.6	63.7	245.3	150.3	34.1	184.4
1. Purchase of Equipment[2]	75.0	44.1	119.1	90.0	10.3	100.3
2. Other Investment[3]	106.6	19.6	126.2	60.3	23.8	84.1
Total	1,252.4	2,058.9	3,311.3	695.0	1,737.8	2,432.8

Source: Banco Central de Reserva del Peru, Economic and Financial Review No. 22, First Quarter 1968, Table VII.
[1] Includes: emergency works in Moquegua and Tacna made by the Irrigations Bureau; National Hydraulics Institute investments and others made through the Ministry of Agriculture.
[2] Includes office and transport equipment, etc.
[3] Includes mainly investments made by the Justice and Government Ministries. Under foreign debt utilization are included one for industrial investment and another for miscellaneous projects.
[4] To convert dollars to soles, an average exchange rate of 30.61 soles per dollar was used.

Case 10: Short Run Stabilization Policy

By June 1967 Peru's balance of payments situation had deteriorated sufficiently to raise serious questions about the possibility of maintaining the exchange rate. In the last five months alone, official reserves had gone down by $25 million, despite contracting short-term loans amounting to some $35 million. Thus the net foreign position had deteriorated by $61 million. In addition, the outlook for government finances was gloomy. The prospective deficit was estimated at between 5000 million and 8000 million soles.

These elements combined to create a crisis of confidence leading to considerable capital flight.

In the discussion of a possible devaluation, two major currents of opinion were apparent. The optimists claimed that a strong rise in the exchange rate combined with restrictive credit measures and fiscal austerity could cure the Peruvian economy quite rapidly of its current ills and start the country growing soundly again. Of course, a stabilization pause would be required, but would not last more than six months to a year. In support of their position, the optimists pointed to past experience, in particular the two-year period 1958–59 during which the exchange rate depreciated by over 40 per cent with most salutary effects: the growth rate reached almost seven per cent during 1960–66, while the increase in the cost of living during 1958–59 was only about half of the size of the devaluation (excluding the normal price trend), thus allowing relative prices to adjust in the correct direction; and a deficit of the balance of payments was converted to a surplus. (See Table 10–1 and Pr.–9.)

The pessimists felt that historical analogy can be dangerous. Substantial structural change had taken place in the economy since the last devaluation, particularly with regard to the composition of imports. The price elasticity of demand for imports was likely to be low, in view of the large share of intermediate goods imports. Thus a major proportion of any devaluation would be nullified by domestic price increases. The pessimists also feared that the supply of exports was not very elastic in the short run in view of the preponderance of minerals in exports. Expanding their supply would require large investments with long gestation periods. The data used by the pessimists is shown in Tables 10–2, 10–3, 10–4, and 10–5.

The Minister feels that a devaluation is unavoidable, if only to reverse the capital flight. He also points out that exchange control is politically not feasible and that import duties have been repeatedly raised in the last years, thus making an additional increase difficult to get through Congress.

To come to a well thought-out decision, the Minister requests a detailed study covering the following points:

1. What would an appropriate new rate be? How long could it be expected to stay in force? (A further devaluation in less than four years is regarded as undesirable.)

2. What would be the consequences of this new rate on the balance of payments, government finances and the price level? (Note that price control is regarded as administratively and politically unfeasible.)

3. Should the new rate be pegged from the start or should it be allowed to drift upwards from the old to the new level?

4. What complementary monetary policy action, if any, is desirable?

5. What complementary fiscal policy, if any, should be adopted?

The authorities wish to have those estimates backed up by proforma statements of the balance of payments, government budget and monetary program.

Table 10–1 *Exchange Rate and Price Movements During Two Lastest Devaluations*

		Exchange Rate	Wholesale Prices	Cost of Living	Prices of Domestic Consumption Goods	Prices of Imported Goods
			1953–54			
1953	Jan.	15.68	849.5	586.9	661.4	896.5
	Feb.	15.89	850.1	587.8	679.6	884.0
	Mar.	15.93	854.7	589.2	658.9	882.0
	Apr.	16.16	855.7	590.0	658.8	877.0
	May	16.34	900.4	634.8	685.3	934.2
	June	16.24	880.4	631.4	681.3	920.1
	July	16.30	890.0	631.5	678.0	926.2
	Aug.	16.85	876.3	629.6	674.1	927.8
	Sept.	17.80	865.9	633.8	671.3	935.3
	Oct.	17.85	874.7	635.9	670.9	932.6
	Nov.	18.72	894.2	635.6	678.4	955.0
	Dec.	19.49	908.4	635.4	686.0	978.4
1954	Jan.	20.99	916.9	638.7	688.1	988.1
	Feb.	19.91	942.1	641.6	711.0	1022.9
	Mar.	19.59	943.7	641.7	716.5	1022.5
	Apr.	19.76	951.8	647.9	716.0	1006.7
	May	19.95	946.6	648.3	725.8	1009.9
	June	19.81	957.4	647.0	731.4	1019.5
	July	19.85	965.2	652.9	740.0	1019.1
	Aug.	19.72	972.1	654.5	757.0	1040.0
	Sept.	19.43	992.9	657.5	766.3	1063.4
	Oct.	19.20	988.2	661.9	784.8	1075.6
	Nov.	19.05	1005.3	664.9	786.0	1076.0
	Dec.	19.01	1002.5	666.1	797.0	1057.4

Table 10–1 (continued)

					Prices of Domestic	*Prices of*
		Exchange Rate	*Wholesale Prices*	*Cost of Living*	*Consumption Goods*	*Imported Goods*
1958	Jan.	19.37	1187.8	797.3	986.7	1139.6
	Feb.	21.90	1209.6	810.5	1052.2	1186.3
	Mar.	22.91	1220.7	816.2	1084.5	1378.3
	Apr.	22.86	1239.0	819.9	1003.6	1235.0
	May	22.72	1245.0	824.3	1011.2	1221.3
	June	23.58	1255.2	831.9	1020.2	1241.4
	July	24.23	1270.5	842.5	1063.6	1176.6
	Aug.	24.12	1283.1	856.5	1065.4	1297.4
	Sept.	24.21	1295.1	851.0	1042.1	1307.4
	Oct.	24.75	1299.1	848.0	1049.0	1349.4
	Nov.	25.10	1321.9	856.8	1058.0	1384.3
	Dec.	25.09	1339.0	860.4	1067.4	1413.5
1959	Jan.	25.27	1348.4	869.4	1082.1	1379.4
	Feb.	26.83	1362.3	874.0	1090.1	1408.3
	Mar.	27.60	1387.2	883.6	1105.7	1420.3
	Apr.	27.52	1418.7	894.5	1143.5	1486.9
	May	27.46	1438.6	906.8	1149.0	1491.9
	June	28.20	1454.9	921.3	1168.5	1573.7
	July	29.11	1511.0	937.7	1202.0	1619.1
	Aug.	28.26	1610.4	995.1	1289.8	1663.8
	Sept.	28.20	1659.0	995.6	1296.3	1702.9
	Oct.	27.75	1683.7	1001.7	1322.2	1823.5
	Nov.	27.72	1696.0	1003.0	1314.2	1757.9
	Dec.	27.71	1708.5	1004.8	1326.8	1735.1
1960	Jan.	27.71	1706.8	1011.6	1336.2	1570.3
	Feb.	27.72	1720.3	1012.0	1345.8	1757.0
	Mar.	27.71	1734.3	1012.4	1337.0	1743.4
	Apr.	27.71	1712.7	1006.2	1329.4	1725.4
	May	27.58	1712.5	1008.4	1338.2	1705.0
	June	27.46	1708.4	1008.5	1352.8	1683.5
	July	27.29	1711.9	1015.8	1358.3	1674.9
	Aug.	26.93	1720.4	1029.4	1359.9	1663.9
	Sept.	26.89	1722.2	1039.3	1341.7	1667.4
	Oct.	26.91	1723.3	1049.2	1356.8	1676.7
	Nov.	26.85	1726.9	1038.9	1353.8	1674.1
	Dec.	26.80	1723.3	1029.4	1363.0	1682.5

1958–60

Source: Boletin del Banco Central de Reserva del Peru, Lima, 1953–1960

Table 10–2 *Peru: Exports, 1950–1966 (Millions of dollars)*

	1950	1951	1952	1953	1954	1955	1956	1957
Cotton								
Value	68.0	85.6	79.3	65.2	64.8	68.1	85.7	67.8
Thousands of Metric Tons	73.6	62.4	82.7	89.6	84.3	85.3	109.0	80.3
Unit Value	924.3	1,372.0	958.3	727.4	768.9	798.8	785.8	844.9
Sugar								
Value	29.7	34.5	33.1	34.7	33.0	37.0	32.8	49.6
Thousands of Metric Tons	290.5	271.3	293.0	424.2	457.7	497.2	428.3	496.3
Unit Value	102.2	127.1	112.9	81.8	72.1	74.3	76.5	99.9
Coffee								
Value	1.0	2.4	2.8	5.3	7.1	8.0	8.9	13.0
Thousands of Metric Tons	1.0	2.2	2.6	4.7	4.7	6.8	7.1	11.1
Unit Value	1,005.7	1,083.6	1,096.8	1,135.8	1,504.7	1,178.5	1,265.6	1,176.4
Wool								
Value	7.9	13.8	7.6	8.7	8.5	5.9	8.0	9.8
Thousands of Metric Tons	7.5	5.5	5.0	5.7	5.2	3.6	5.4	6.6
Unit Value	1,062.7	2,504.8	1,511.4	1,512.7	1,623.9	1,621.7	1,471.3	1,490.9
Fish and Subproducts								
Value	5.7	6.1	7.8	7.0	11.2	11.8	14.9	18.4
Thousands of Metric Tons	21.6	23.5	30.0	27.7	40.6	47.3	61.0	97.7
Unit Value	265.9	257.3	260.3	251.1	274.8	248.7	244.9	188.4
Petroleum and Subproducts								
Value	25.3	20.6	17.3	14.4	17.1	22.1	23.8	26.8
Thousands of Metric Tons	1,031.2	1,032.5	963.8	724.9	778.2	905.0	1,017.9	1,040.1
Unit Value	24.5	19.9	17.9	19.8	21.9	24.4	23.5	25.7

Table 10–2 (continued)

	1958	1959	1960	1961	1962	1963	1964	1965	1966
Cotton									
Value	75.2	69.2	73.1	79.3	97.1	91.3	91.2	87.4	85.4
Thousands of Metric Tons	110.6	113.9	99.0	113.0	139.6	124.6	115.1	115.8	114.9
Unit Value	680.5	607.8	738.1	701.5	695.6	732.3	792.3	755.0	743.1
Sugar									
Value	33.9	35.9	47.5	63.9	53.8	63.1	63.5	36.8	46.3
Thousands of Metric Tons	410.7	437.0	525.8	556.5	478.6	495.8	424.8	365.6	429.9
Unit Value	82.6	82.1	90.3	114.8	112.5	127.4	149.4	100.8	107.8
Coffee									
Value	15.8	15.6	18.6	22.8	24.2	25.6	37.0	29.0	28.5
Thousands of Metric Tons	17.3	19.9	26.4	34.0	37.4	40.1	42.3	34.6	35.4
Unit Value	909.9	784.5	702.3	669.6	646.2	638.0	875.1	839.4	805.5
Wool									
Value	6.0	9.0	7.1	7.4	8.9	11.7	11.6	9.1	8.3
Thousands of Metric Tons	4.9	7.8	5.0	5.0	6.5	8.4	7.2	4.9	5.3
Unit Value	1,228.2	1,244.5	1,398.0	1,498.6	1,360.3	1,395.6	1,598.4	1,860.7	1,544.5
Fish and Subproducts									
Value	17.9	42.5	50.0	69.7	119.8	120.2	165.7	185.7	205.7
Thousands of Metric Tons	137.2	338.5	575.4	849.9	1,219.5	1,199.7	1,565.5	1,581.4	1,421.7
Unit Value	130.4	125.7	86.9	82.1	98.2	100.2	105.8	117.4	144.7
Petroleum and Subproducts									
Value	16.5	16.1	17.9	14.5	13.2	9.8	9.6	9.3	7.4
Thousands of Metric Tons	702.6	651.0	786.1	685.3	623.0	509.4	499.3	472.2	371.8
Unit Value	23.5	24.7	22.8	21.1	21.1	19.3	19.3	19.6	19.9

Table 10–2 (continued)

	1950	1951	1952	1953	1954	1955	1956	1957	1958
Copper									
Value	10.2	15.3	17.1	17.4	20.0	29.3	33.6	24.5	20.0
Thousands of Metric Tons	27.2	33.8	32.5	31.9	37.5	41.3	44.0	50.6	53.9
Unit Value	373.2	451.1	529.1	547.2	533.6	708.8	764.3	483.9	408.7
Silver									
Value	8.0	10.4	12.4	11.7	14.4	16.2	17.7	17.9	18.9
Thousands of Metric Tons	383.6	421.8	504.7	488.2	597.0	631.6	661.3	653.4	758.5
Unit Value	20.8	24.7	24.5	24.0	24.1	25.6	26.7	27.4	24.9
Lead									
Value	12.3	23.6	23.9	22.5	23.7	26.2	31.3	29.3	24.4
Thousands of Metric Tons	60.3	82.0	90.2	105.6	107.1	107.1	120.9	119.6	136.4
Unit Value	203.7	288.0	265.4	213.5	221.2	244.2	258.6	244.9	178.9
Zinc									
Value	10.3	15.1	15.0	7.6	9.1	13.8	14.1	15.1	11.3
Thousands of Metric Tons	63.6	99.1	113.0	97.6	112.5	146.6	143.9	146.6	136.6
Unit Value	161.4	152.9	133.2	78.1	80.5	94.3	98.2	102.7	82.6
Iron Ore									
Value	—	—	—	6.4	12.9	8.0	14.8	23.4	16.4
Thousands of Metric Tons	—	—	—	553.2	1,169.3	1,019.3	1,629.7	2,226.8	1,524.0
Unit Value	—	—	—	11.5	11.1	7.9	9.1	10.5	10.8
Other Products	15.2	25.1	22.4	21.1	25.8	24.5	25.8	34.4	36.1
Total Exports FOB	193.6	252.5	238.7	222.0	247.6	270.9	311.4	330.0	292.4

Table 10-2 *(continued)*

	1959	1960	1961	1962	1963	1964	1965	1966
Copper								
Value	24.9	94.7	105.1	92.4	87.3	103.2	120.9	186.2
Thousands of Metric Tons	48.9	168.0	198.8	171.9	163.4	179.7	179.8	176.1
Unit Value	509.4	563.6	528.8	537.4	534.2	574.5	672.4	1,057.3
Silver								
Value	20.4	24.2	27.6	33.0	35.8	45.3	39.1	41.4
Thousands of Metric Tons	835.5	926.5	1,035.2	1,069.6	983.2	1,152.3	1,027.8	1,100.1
Unit Value	24.4	26.1	26.6	30.8	36.4	39.3	38.0	37.7
Lead								
Value	21.2	21.7	22.3	16.3	16.4	33.0	37.9	34.6
Thousands of Metric Tons	115.1	117.8	142.5	135.2	120.5	166.7	151.0	150.9
Unit Value	183.8	184.0	156.5	120.3	136.1	197.8	250.8	229.3
Zinc								
Value	14.1	16.7	19.1	15.8	15.8	39.1	35.9	34.0
Thousands of Metric Tons	156.6	157.8	206.5	181.7	186.9	275.0	267.7	282.2
Unit Value	90.4	106.0	92.3	87.1	84.7	142.2	134.2	120.6
Iron Ore								
Value	19.4	32.7	36.8	32.7	36.4	38.9	47.0	53.4
Thousands of Metric Tons	2,016.4	3,124.9	3,381.7	3,149.0	3,579.7	3,709.9	4,594.2	4,858.7
Unit Value	9.6	10.5	10.9	10.4	10.2	10.5	10.2	11.0
Other Products	26.7	29.0	27.9	32.8	27.8	28.9	29.2	33.1
Total Exports FOB	315.0	433.1	496.4	540.0	541.2	667.0	667.3	764.3

Source: Banco Central de Reserva del Peru, *Cuentas Nacionales del Peru, 1950–67*, Lima 1968.
Note: The values in this table are taken from the Customs Statistics and do not include the adjustments made when computing the Balance of Payments.

Table 10-3 Peru: Imports—1950–1965 (Thousands of dollars)

	1950	1951	1952	1953	1954	1955	1956	1957	1958
1. Non Durable Consumption Goods	27,369	35,435	38,817	34,159	33,411	40,293	42,893	54,066	54,325
Food	16,845	18,302	22,076	16,757	16,599	20,659	22,661	29,129	32,635
2. Durable Consumption Goods	15,115	35,239	31,349	31,876	20,925	32,277	43,041	46,802	36,123
3. Fuel, Lubricants	3,537	6,420	4,706	4,836	6,440	9,346	12,069	15,845	11,585
4. Raw Materials & Intermediate Products for Agriculture	1,773	3,381	4,118	3,583	4,323	6,539	5,120	5,994	8,084
5. Raw Materials & Intermediate Products for Industry (exclusive of construction)	64,189	91,931	100,321	95,330	86,887	102,455	113,691	131,168	108,693
6. Construction Material	6,747	14,337	18,688	22,816	15,094	20,748	27,119	31,467	28,603
7. Capital Goods for Agriculture	7,478	10,396	12,418	12,306	9,879	11,133	12,836	16,466	14,506
8. Capital Goods for Industry	28,162	39,751	53,299	59,653	47,778	54,667	84,387	96,043	86,265
9. Transport Equipment	20,225	23,610	21,974	25,820	21,572	19,484	35,992	49,039	33,470
10. Others, n.e.s.	1,034	1,416	1,859	2,444	3,381	2,573	6,819	2,534	3,001
Total	175,629	261,916	287,549	292,823	249,690	299,515	383,967	449,424	384,655

Table 10–3 (continued)

	1959	1960	1961	1962	1963	1964	1965 Old[1]	1965 New[2]	1966
1. Non Durable Consumption Goods	43,684	45,289	51,815	52,258	56,130	69,700	85,108	83,831	80,452
Food	23,670	22,945	24,647	24,737	27,814	40,045	54,995	—	—
2. Durable Consumption Goods	25,829	35,008	47,616	47,917	58,196	63,884	63,033	65,627	70,098
3. Fuel, Lubricants	12,574	17,201	15,650	16,430	15,620	18,250	20,518	20,518	25,222
4. Raw Materials & Intermediate Products for Agriculture	8,219	9,415	10,007	10,418	9,389	10,775	14,061	14,066	11,175
5. Raw Materials & Intermediate Products for Industry (exclusive of construction)	107,995	129,619	160,497	180,627	200,175	193,556	264,843	289,252	335,574
6. Construction Material	12,227	13,831	20,054	24,828	18,649	21,160	29,513	27,057	28,639
7. Capital Goods for Agriculture	8,146	10,762	14,038	14,591	14,809	14,794	19,026	19,052	24,805
8. Capital Goods for Industry	60,558	71,351	96,430	142,231	145,273	138,358	169,171	135,891	171,269
9. Transport Equipment	35,342	38,718	50,509	52,144	58,433	54,345	65,839	62,204	66,976
10. Others, n.e.s.	2,120	1,579	1,491	1,477	1,861	2,291	2,525	1,123	2,509
Total	316,694	372,773	468,107	542,921	578,535	587,113	733,637	718,621	816,719

Source: Banco Central de Reserva del Peru, *Cuentas Nacionales del Peru*, 1950–1965 (1966), 1950–1967 (1968).
[1] Based on "old" tariff classification.
[2] Based on "new" tariff classification.

Table 10–4 Peru: Composition of Imports 1950–1966 (Per cent)

	1950	1951	1952	1953	1954	1955	1956	1957	1958
Non Durable Consumption Goods	15.6	13.5	13.5	11.7	13.4	13.5	11.2	12.0	14.1
Durable Consumption Goods	8.6	13.4	10.9	10.9	8.4	10.8	11.2	10.4	9.4
Fuel, Lubricants	2.0	2.5	1.6	1.7	2.6	3.1	3.1	3.5	3.0
Raw Materials & Intermediate Products for Agriculture	1.0	1.3	1.4	1.2	1.7	2.2	1.3	1.3	2.1
Raw Materials & Intermediate Products for Industry (exclusive of construction)	36.5	35.1	34.9	32.6	34.8	34.2	29.6	29.2	28.3
Construction Material	3.8	5.5	6.5	7.8	6.0	6.9	7.1	7.0	7.4
Capital Goods for Agriculture	4.3	4.0	4.3	4.2	4.0	3.7	3.3	3.7	3.8
Capital Goods for Industry	16.0	15.2	18.5	20.4	19.1	18.3	22.0	21.4	22.4
Transport Equipment	11.5	9.0	7.6	8.8	8.6	6.5	9.4	10.9	8.7
Others, n.e.s.	.6	.5	.6	.8	1.4	.9	1.8	.6	.8
Total	100.0	100.0	100.0	100.0	100.0	100.0	100.0	100.0	100.0

Table 10–4 *(continued)*

	1959	1960	1961	1962	1963	1964	1965 Old[1]	1965 New[2]	1966
Non Durable Consumption Goods	13.8	12.2	11.1	9.6	9.7	11.9	11.6	11.7	9.8
Durable Consumption Goods	8.2	9.4	10.2	8.8	10.1	10.9	8.6	9.1	8.6
Fuel, Lubricants	4.0	4.6	3.3	3.0	2.7	3.1	2.8	2.9	3.1
Raw Materials & Intermediate Products for Agriculture	2.6	2.5	2.1	1.9	1.6	1.8	1.9	2.0	1.4
Raw Materials & Intermediate Products for Industry (exclusive of construction)	34.1	34.8	34.3	33.3	34.6	33.0	36.1	40.3	41.1
Construction Material	3.9	3.7	4.3	4.6	3.2	3.6	4.0	3.8	3.5
Capital Goods for Agriculture	2.6	2.9	3.0	2.7	2.6	2.5	2.6	2.7	3.0
Capital Goods for Industry	19.1	19.1	20.6	26.2	25.1	23.6	23.1	18.9	21.0
Transport Equipment	11.2	10.4	10.8	9.6	10.1	9.3	9.0	8.7	8.2
Others, n.e.s.	.7	.4	.3	.3	.3	.4	.3	.2	.3
Total	100.0	100.0	100.0	100.0	100.0	100.0	100.0	100.0	100.0

Source: Banco Central de Reserva del Peru, *Cuentas Nacionales del Peru, 1950–1967* (1968), 1950–1965 (1966).
[1] Based on the "old" tariff classification.
[2] Based on the "new" tariff classification.

Table 10–5   Peru: Production and Import of Food, 1963–1966
(Millions of soles at 1963 prices)

		1963	1964	1965	1966
1.	Production				
	Rice	586	763	630	754
	Sugar	918	958	1,064	1,056
	Potatoes	2,183	2,343	2,399	2,320
	Fruit	1,276	1,365	1,497	1,515
	Corn	468	490	576	663
	Wheat	1,945	2,103	2,036	2,172
	Fresh Milk	1,572	1,637	1,667	1,702
	Others	2,632	2,706	2,769	2,778
	Total	11,580	12,365	12,638	12,964
2.	Imports				
	Wheat	770	833	980	1,042
	Meat	645	350	475	695
	Oils & Fats	295	441	353	547
	Milk	222	297	328	403
	Rice	5	197	377	48
	Others	221	228	229	246
	Total	2,158	2,346	2,742	2,981
3.	Grand Total	13,738	14,711	15,380	15,945
4.	Imported Supply	15.7%	15.9%	7.8%	18.7%

Source: Banco Central de Reserva del Peru, Reseña Economica y Financiera, Second Trimestr, pp. 17, 18.

Table 10–6   Expenditure Weights Used to Compute the Cost of Living for Peru;
1934–36, 1960 and 1966

	Expenditure weights			
	1934–36	1960		1966
Expenditure group		Blue collar	White collar	
Total expenditures	100.0	100.0	100.0	100.00
Food and beverages	55.00	55.61	47.04	51.80
Cereals and derivatives	7.98	10.63	8.75	9.50
Bread	5.50			
Meat and meat preparations	14.03	18.96	17.68	13.60
Seafood				2.00
Edible fats and oils	3.12	2.08	1.27	3.60
Dairy products and eggs	6.93	2.04	5.72	6.40
Fresh vegetables		4.80	2.83	3.70
Tubers	7.92	4.16	2.54	2.40
Fresh fruits		3.75	2.74	2.60
Pulses and derivatives	2.42	3.51	0.82	1.50

Table 10–6 (continued)

Expenditure group	1934–36	1960 Blue collar	1960 White collar	1966
		Expenditure weights		
Sugar, salt and spices	2.26	2.69	1.97	2.30
Other food products				0.40
Cooking fuel	3.30	—	—	—
Non-alcoholic beverages	1.54	1.94	2.20	2.10
Alcoholic beverages				0.60
Food and beverages consumed outside the home	—	1.05	0.52	1.10
Housing and furniture	18.00	18.51	21.31	21.00
Rent	—	10.61	14.32	11.10
Apartments	10.80	—	—	—
Private housing	4.50	—	—	—
Employee housing	2.70	—	—	—
Real estate taxes	—	—	—	0.40
Municipal utilities	—	—	—	0.50
Electricity and gas	—	2.04	1.60	2.70
Household fabrics	—	2.98	2.90	0.80
Household furniture	—	—	—	1.20
Kitchen utensils	—	1.15	1.15	0.50
Kitchen equipment	—			0.90
Other household articles	—	1.73	1.34	0.60
Cleaning and maintenance	—	—	—	2.30
Clothing	12.00	10.07	12.32	12.30
Male adult	4.47	4.15	5.07	5.60
Male child	1.96	1.40	1.40	—
Female adult	2.44	2.68	4.00	4.70
Female child	2.53	0.90	0.90	
Children less than 2 years	—	0.13	0.14	0.30
Cloth, tailoring and laundry	—	—	—	1.70
Other	0.60	0.81	0.81	—
Other	15.00	15.81	19.33	14.90
Health care	0.75	1.74	1.80	1.50
Personal hygene	0.39	1.99	2.60	3.50
Recreation and reading materials	2.93	1.79	2.67	2.40
Tobacco	0.45	—	—	0.70
Other beverages	0.75	1.86	2.38	—
Transportation	4.80	7.48	8.55	2.90
Education and culture	2.56	0.95	1.33	2.10
Automobile and related expenses	—	—	—	0.10
Other	2.37	—	—	1.30

Source: Direccion Nacional de Estadistica y Censos. I.N.P.

Macroeconomic Planning

Introduction

Perhaps the most difficult problem faced by development economists is the devising of a reasonably effective and consistent overall development strategy. It may also be the most important problem.

One of the crucial aspects of such a strategy is the decision taken with respect to the internal terms of trade of an economy. In dealing with the balance of payments the more familiar external terms of trade play an important role, but largely as a datum, a given, an exogenous factor. Policy makers in most countries can have only limited effects on that country's terms of trade. But the internal terms of trade, particularly the prices at which agriculture and industry exchange their products are both important and often subject to policy influence over a wide range. Price and trade policy for agriculture is an important aspect of policy with respect to internal terms of trade, especially in the late 1960s when several important less developed countries rather suddenly find that agricultural output is increasing quite substantially. Unfortunately, one of the most promising tools for strategy decisions, the macro-model, is not particularly helpful for this set of decisions. Most models assume fixed prices or fixed price relationships, since even on that simplifying assumption they are already complex enough.

There has been a macro-model explosion in the last decade. Many have been designed, and have proved most helpful, in answering questions on the consistency of broad plan aggregates—for example, are targets consistent with assumptions about capital output ratios in different sectors, savings rates and foreign aid inflows, export earnings projections and government fiscal policy. The construction of formal planning models has moved far ahead of their application to actual planning problems and models, like other new ideas and techniques, have their evangelists. Government officials therefore find that they need to decide first whether to use a formal planning model or to rely in the more traditional casual check of consistency which can be done on a scratch pad even if not on the proverbial back of an envelope. More important, they have to decide how complex a model they should try to construct. If it is too simple, too naive, it will not generate many useful answers; if it is too complex the results it provides may be very hard to interpret and besides a complex model may swallow too much scarce manpower and be operational only after all decisions have been made.

Macro-models have also been less useful in dealing with priority, as distinguished from consistency, decisions. Yet broad strategy questions on the sectors and locations which are to be given priority in development, on the extent of government and private initiative, and on the trade-off between growth and equity are among the most contentious in development. At the moment there are few good answers to these questions. Political factors tend to play a major role in decisions. But economic analysis is beginning to contribute to the decisions and it is appropriate to end an examination of important policy decisions in development with the contribution of economic analysis to the profound but difficult and fuzzy question of development strategy.

Case 11: Agricultural Policies and the Internal Terms of Trade: "The Green Revolution"

The agricultural program in West Pakistan during the Third Five-Year Plan period (1965/66–1969/70) has been a success. The targets set for the agricultural sector in that province will, in all likelihood, not only be achieved but surpassed, especially in regard to foodgrains. It would thus appear that the transformation of agriculture from a tradition bound and lagging sector to a rapidly growing one, a change which many development economists consider a necessary precondition for development, may have been achieved. One might expect such success to be greeted with unmitigated joy by the policy makers. On closer examination, however, it appears that the very policies responsible for the "green revolution" raise a number of new issues which must be resolved before an agricultural policy can be formulated for the Fourth Plan. To appreciate more fully the issues involved, it is necessary to review briefly the past policies and their impact.

During the Second Five-Year Plan period (1960/61–1964/65) the agriculture sector in West Pakistan grew at an annual rate of 3.8 per cent compared to a rate of 2.1 per cent in the previous five year period. Even more dramatic was the performance in certain subsectors of agriculture, including wheat and other cereals and especially rice production, which grew at an annual rate of 7.8 per cent. (See Table 11–2.)

A careful analysis of the impact and availability of new inputs showed that the growth in agricultural output was not simply due to "favorable weather" but represented a major shift in the production function. Prior to 1957/58, individual farmers could do little to supplement their meager water supply, an essential input into agriculture in West Pakistan where nearly 75 per cent of the wheat and 90 per cent of the rice is grown on irrigated lands. Although no major changes were made in the existing canal irrigation system, the Department of Agriculture did sink a limited number of tubewells.[1] These tubewells helped spread a new technology which was vital for agricultural development. Farmers soon realized that the availability of extra tubewell water had a very high marginal-value product.[2]

Although the general profitability of tubewells was one major reason for their rapid spread (nearly 7,000 were installed in 1963/64), public policy aided this process. The profitability of tubewells was increased by government price policy aimed at stabilizing agricultural prices at a relatively high level. The import liberalization program, begun during the latter part of

[1] See Ghulam Mohammed, "Private Tubewell Development and Cropping Patterns in West Pakistan," *Pakistan Development Review,* vol. 5 (Spring 1965) pp. 1–53.

[2] Estimates of the value of water, derived from various linear programming models range from Rs. 97 per acre/foot to Rs. 188 per acre/foot. Regardless of which estimate one accepts, the benefits from additional water greatly exceeded its cost. It has been estimated that the investment payout period for a tubewell was *less than two years.*

the 1960s, permitted the raw materials for the construction of tubewells to be purchased freely and at a price which was lower than the opportunity cost of foreign exchange. In addition the price for electricity and diesel fuel, which provide the motive power for the tubewells, has been kept low. Private tubewells increased the water supply to agriculture in West Pakistan by 9 per cent and contributed 25 per cent of the increase in the value of crop output.[3] In addition, the increased and more flexible water supplies helped to induce the use of other modern inputs, especially fertilizer.

Fertilizer is the second most important variable in explaining the growth performance of agriculture in the Second Plan. Again, government policies had a profound impact on the use of this input. In 1960/61, 31 thousand nutrient tons[4] were used; by 1964/65, fertilizer use, in terms of nutrient tons, had nearly tripled. The use of fertilizers was stimulated by a 50 per cent subsidy on the price of fertilizer (see Table 11–3). In addition, the distribution system for fertilizers was greatly improved by allowing private stocklists to handle sales. As domestic fertilizer production was insufficient to meet demand, considerable foreign exchange was made available for the import of fertilizer. It is estimated that fertilizer by itself accounted for about one per cent of gross annual increase in crop production in West Pakistan during the Second Plan.[5] (That is, one-fifth of the total increase, which averaged five per cent per year.)

Two other major sources of increased output should be noted. First, plant protection measures were applied to approximately six million acres of crops at a 100 per cent subsidy. And during the Second Plan a beginning was made on the introduction of new imported seeds, especially for wheat (Mexi-Pak), rice (IRRI), and maize. A summary of the various factors that contributed to the increased growth of agricultural production over the period 1960/61–1964/65 is shown in Table 11–4.

During the Third Plan period the basic agricultural strategy, with its emphasis on subsidizing inputs continued although in West Pakistan the subsidy on fertilizer was reduced from 50 to 35 per cent, and on pesticides from 100 to 75 per cent. In addition the government has continued its efforts to distribute the new seed varieties. In 1967/68, the government announced support prices for rice, wheat, and maize. These support prices (see Table 11–5) are to be maintained at least until 1969/70, the end of the Third Plan. In 1967/68, the Government for the first time entered the market as a major buyer of wheat in order to maintain the support price.

The effect of these agricultural policies has clearly been profound. Yet the very success of these policies raises a number of new issues. It is likely

---

[3] Walter P. Falcon and Carl H. Gotsch, "Lessons in Agricultural Development—Pakistan" in G. F. Papanek, ed. *Development Policy: Theory and Practice* (Cambridge: Harvard University Press, 1968), pp. 277–8.

[4] Nutrient tons refer to tons of nitrogen in the various forms of fertilizer.

[5] Falcon and Gotsch, "Lessons in Agricultural Development—Pakistan," p. 282.

that West Pakistan will have an export surplus of rice and wheat and almost certainly of maize. The forecast is for an output of 7 million tons of wheat in 1969/70 and 10.5 million tons in 1974/75. For rice, the forecast output level is 2.1 million tons in 1969/70 and 3.5 million tons in 1974/75. Although the precise magnitude of the exportable surplus is not yet known, given the recent domestic and international price levels (see Table 11–5), the sale of West Pakistan's agricultural surplus on the export market will not be a routine matter.

While West Pakistan may have an exportable surplus of both rice and wheat it is very likely that East Pakistan will continue to be a food deficit region for some time. The possibility of exporting food grains from one region and the need to import food grains into another raises a number of complex policy issues. One possibility is to ship the exportable surplus produced by West Pakistan to meet the needs of East Pakistan's population. The shipping cost of doing so is approximately $10 per ton. A second possibility is to sell West Pakistan's surplus on the international market and to meet the import demand for East Pakistan by buying food grains in the world market. An evaluation of these alternatives requires an analysis of a number of issues.

In the past, while Pakistan was a food deficit country, it imported agricultural commodities from the U.S. at concessional rates under the PL 480 program (see Table 11–6). These PL 480 commodity imports have provided the government not only with additional physical resources but with financial resources as the government sold the PL 480 commodities to the consumers. PL 480 counterpart rupees financed nearly ten per cent of the Second Plan development expenditure,[6] and were expected to finance nearly eight per cent of development expenditure in the Third Plan.[7] Under the "like-commodity" clause a country cannot obtain PL 480 commodities if it exports the same commodities. At present the Planning Commission is considering the possibility of importing wheat from the United States. If Pakistan also wishes to export rice it may be required to offset each ton of rice exported by the purchase of a ton of wheat from the U.S. on commercial terms. (Pakistan has in the past exported a high quality of rice which was excluded from the PL 480 "like-commodity" clause. While exports of such basmati rice can of course continue, problems arise because the new IRRI rice varieties are considered a "like-commodity" with U.S. PL 480 food grain imports including wheat.) The cost of wheat from the U.S. is $56 per ton fob and $80 per ton cif. The purchase of these commodities would be financed by a loan that has a ten year grace period during which the interest rate is 2.5 per cent and a 30 year repayment period with a 3 per cent interest rate. Sixty per cent of the loan would be repaid in dollars and forty per cent

[6] Planning Commission, Government of Pakistan, *Evaluation of the Second Five-Year Plan (1960–65)* (Karachi: May 1966), p. 19.

[7] Planning Commission, Government of Pakistan, *The Third Five-Year Plan (1965–70)* (Karachi, June 1965), p. 66.

in rupees. Furthermore twenty per cent of the rupees would be for the United States' "own" uses to cover the costs of its Embassy and so on. The remainder of the rupees are likely to be relent to Pakistan for development purposes. Half of the shipping charges would be financed by a dollar loan on terms similar to the PL 480 loan, the other half by Pakistan, mostly in foreign exchange. Clearly then any decision to import PL 480 commodities from the United States will depend on its "real" cost.

It will also be necessary to estimate the quantity of food imports required by East Pakistan. This in turn will depend on the size of the population and the level of agricultural production in the province, and on the price for rice.[8] Table 11–11 shows the yearly average price for rice in East Pakistan. A recent analysis[9] has established the following relationship between the level of rice production, food grain imports, and the price level in East Pakistan:

$$dP = 3.30 - 7.08 \frac{dI}{I_t} - 67.33 \frac{dR}{R_t}$$

where:

dP = change in the price of rice, expressed as Rs./mnd. (rupees per maund)

$\dfrac{dI}{I_t}$ = fractional change in *food grain* imports

$\dfrac{dR}{R_t}$ = fractional change in production of domestic rice.

Imports of foodgrains were approximately 1.1 million tons in 1968/69 while Table 11–12 shows the rice production in East Pakistan since 1955/56. (Changes in wheat and other food grain production in East Pakistan are not significant.)

Finally, the use of the new seed varieties has altered the cropping pattern in West Pakistan (see Figure 11–1 with accompanying notes). One possible effect is to permit West Pakistani farmers greater flexibility in shifting between crops in response to relative prices. Hence future agricultural policies will have to pay greater attention to the question of relative prices of agriculture commodities.

In drafting an agricultural program for the Fourth Plan the government needs advice on the following issues:

1. What is the likely exportable surplus for wheat and rice from West Pakistan over the longer run (say to 1975)? It has been estimated that

---

[8] For a number of reasons the government has always sold wheat in East Pakistan at a fixed highly subsidized price. Hence the retail price of wheat need not be considered a variable in the analysis.

[9] A. K. M. Ghulam Rabbani and R. C. Repetto, "Foodgrains Availability, Money Supply, and the Price Level in East Pakistan: Some Simple Econometrics of Short-Term Stabilization Policies," *Pakistan Development Review*, vol. 7 (Summer 1968) pp. 281–287.

the (per capita) expenditure elasticity of demand for wheat in West Pakistan is 0.38 and for rice is 0.80. The price elasticity is taken to be −0.55.

2. Is it desirable to continue the present price policy on inputs and outputs for agriculture? If the present policy is to be changed, how is this change to be brought about? (Although it would be desirable to have information on the likely elasticities of supply, few data are available which would allow one to estimate such a parameter.) What are the likely consequences of a change in price policies on savings, investment, wages, output, government revenues and government expenditures?

3. What is the likely range of the foodgrain deficit in East Pakistan? How should this deficit be met? If there is to be a sale of wheat and/or rice from West to East Pakistan, at what price should such sales take place? At the West Pakistan support price? The East Pakistan release price for wheat (Rs 17.50/mnd)? Or at the "world market" price? What would be the effects of different price policies on development in the two Provinces? Note that there is an urgent political, social and economic need to reduce the rice prices in East Pakistan substantially below the 1968/69 level.

4. If PL 480 imports of rice and wheat are stopped, how are the fiscal resources which the government previously obtained from the sale of PL 480 commodities to be replaced?

5. Considering all the foregoing factors, what prices should the government guarantee for West Pakistan's wheat and rice? Will there be a surplus for export at that price? What steps, if any, would be required so that exports actually take place?

The Planning Commission is acutely aware that the decision it must make in regard to the agricultural sector will not only have an economic impact but major political implications as well. Hence, it requires a full analysis of the various likely effects of alternative policy recommendations.

Table 11–1   *Third Agricultural Targets and Achievements—West Pakistan*

Commodity	Unit	Third Plan Target (for 1969/70)	1965/66	1966/67	1967/68	Per Cent of Target Achieved
1. Wheat	1,000 tons	5,400	3,854	4,266	6,000	111.1
2. Rice	1,000 tons	1,720	1,296	1,343	1,400	81.4
3. Maize	1,000 tons	770	531	578	779	101.2
4. Other foodgrains	1,000 tons	750	716	725	600	80.0
5. Total	1,000 tons	8,640	6,397	6,912	8,779	101.6
6. Oilseeds	1,000 tons	1,550	1,034	1,147	—	—
7. Sugarcane	1,000 tons	21,250	21,957	21,635	—	—
8. Cotton	10,000 bales	3,500	2,331	2,558	2,700	77.1
9. Tobacco	mill. lbs.	195	243	308	—	—

Source: Planning Commission, Government of Pakistan. *Annual Plan* 1968–69, p. 88

Table 11–2   *Growth of Agriculture in West Pakistan—1959/60–1964/65*

A. Growth of Value Added (1959/60 prices)	
Item	*Per cent per annum[a]*
Total agriculture	3.8
Major crops	4.9
Minor crops	4.8
Livestock	1.9
Forestry	3.9
Fishery	9.7
B. Growth of Crop Production	
Rice	7.8
Wheat	3.7
Bajra	6.9
Jowar	3.7
Maize	3.4
Barley	−6.2
Sugarcane	10.6
Cotton	7.1
Tobacco	6.7

Source: Walter P. Falcon and Carl H. Gotsch, "Lessons in Agricultural Development—Pakistan," Reprinted by permission of the publishers from Gustav F. Papanek, ed. *Development Policy: Theory and Practice* Cambridge, Mass.: Harvard University Press, Copyright, 1968, by the President and Fellows of Harvard College, pp. 271–272.
[a] Least square estimate of "*b*" in log $y = a + b$ time.

Table 11–3   *West Pakistan Fertilizer Consumption, Production and Imports*

Year	Production	Imports[a]	Consumption
		(1000's of nutrient tons)	
1954/55	—	13.0	13.0
1955/56	—	6.0	6.0
1956/57	—	8.0	8.0
1957/58	0.3	15.7	16.0
1958/59	7.8	10.2	18.0
1959/60	9.0	10.4	19.4
1960/61	11.4	20.0	31.4
1961/62	15.1	22.4	37.5
1962/63	41.6	1.4	40.2
1963/64	45.5	23.2	68.7
1964/65	48.5	38.7	87.2
1965/66	n.a.	n.a.	82.0
1966/67	51.9	62.4	114.3
1967/68[b]	55.0	135.0	190.0[c]
1968/69[b]	104.0	236.0	340.0[c]

Sources: Production: Central Statistical Office, Government of Pakistan, *Statistical Bulletin*, various issues.
Consumption: US/AID: *Pakistan Fertilizer Targets 1967–1972.*
n.a. = not available.
[a] Changes in stocks are not available. Imports are defined as the difference between consumption and production.
[b] Estimates based on past capacity plus expected operation of new plants.
[c] Targets.

Table 11–4   *Sources of Increased Crop Output West Pakistan, 1960/61–1964/65*

Source	Per cent per annum
Private tubewells	1.4
Public tubewells	0.6
Surface water	0.7
Fertilizer	1.0
Plant protection	0.4
Seeds	0.2
Others	0.6
Total growth	4.9

Source: Walter P. Falcon and Carl H. Gotsch, "Lessons in Agricultural Development—Pakistan." Reprinted by permission of the publishers from Gustav F. Papanek, ed. *Development Policy: Theory and Practice* Cambridge, Mass.: Harvard University Press, Copyright, 1968, by the President and Fellows of Harvard College, p. 287.

Table 11–5   *Domestic and World Market Prices for Wheat, Rice, and Maize (Rs./mnd.)*

Commodity	Domestic Price Primary Mkt.[1]	FOB Karachi	World Price[2]
1. Wheat	17.00	20.00	12.00
2. IRRI rice	19.00	21.50	13.50
3. Maize	14.50	16.50	7.00

[1] Government announced support price. See, Planning Commission, Government of Pakistan. *Annual Plan*, 1968–1969, p. 43.
[2] At official exchange rate, fob Karachi. One maund equals 82.29 lbs.

Table 11–6   *PL 480 Title I Imports—By Commodity (Rs. millions)*

Year	Wheat	Rice	Edible Oils	Cotton	Tobacco	Others[1]	Total
1955/56	—	—	2.27	23.92	8.19	—	34.38
1956/57	125.15	166.56	0.49	89.88	9.06	3.76	394.90
1957/58	194.17	105.03	11.53	11.85	5.28	5.53	333.39
1958/59	146.64	21.97	7.26	11.23	—	12.28	199.38
1959/60	301.66	23.18	43.78	5.32	—	.82	374.76
1960/61	347.31	66.77	—	7.00	7.59	61.66	489.78
1961/62	228.85	1.65	46.50	26.66	11.76	5.82	321.24
1962/63	428.21	—	142.41	18.09	11.90	25.77	626.38
1963/64	500.19	—	102.13	14.17	9.06	36.70	662.25
1964/65	565.75	—	150.19	2.80	1.06	54.96	774.76
1965/66	278.88	—	142.02	6.99	10.12	8.16	446.17
1966/67	356.37	—	50.50	—	3.13	23.98	433.98

Source: U.S. AID, *Statistical Fact Book*, Karachi, 1968.
[1] Includes corn, dairy products, dried eggs, frozen poultry, and tallow.

Table 11–7 Budget Receipts of Central and Provincial Governments of Pakistan (Rs. millions)

	1959–60	1960–61	1961–62	1962–63	1963–64	1964–65	1965–66
Central Gov't							
Customs	562	588	669	736	704	1030	1051
Central excise	286	344	368	413	606	697	823
Income tax + Corp. tax	320	321	385	280	310	342	280
Sales tax	170	247	255	244	257	269	346
Others	640	623	640	373	953	963	1862
Total Revenue	1978	2123	2317	2046	2830	3301	4362
East Pakistan							
Customs	48	33	62	46	44	27	14
Central excise	22	28	27	51	61	60	89
Corporation tax	—	—	—	67	40	44	75
Tax on income (other than corp. tax)	37	39	44	106	125	135	190
Sales tax	34	52	62	140	187	203	200
Land revenue	94	107	146	77	128	122	134
Irrigation	—	—	—	—	—	—	—
Grants in aid, Foreign aid	4	39	66	69	79	126	70
Others	161	192	218	189	331	430	407
Total Revenue	400	490	625	745	995	1147	1179
West Pakistan							
Customs	—	—	—	41	38	21	11
Central excise duties	23	31	25	43	52	59	74
Corporation tax	—	—	—	23	37	39	48
Taxes on income (other than corp. tax)	29	35	43	79	99	109	147
Sales tax	111	169	175	168	220	235	244
Irrigation	85	106	218	50	74	116	114
Grants in aid from Central Gvt.	31	24	241	222	219	223	193
Others	526	482	382	723	833	911	840
Total Revenue	805	847	1084	1349	1572	1713	1671

Source: Pakistan Economic Survey 1966–67 and 1967–68.

Table 11–8 *Per Capita Availability of Wheat and Rice in West Pakistan*

		1960/61	1961/62	1962/63	1963/64	1964/65	1965/66	1966/67
A.	*Wheat:*							
	1. Official Production (mill. tons)	3.754	3.963	4.104	4.096	4.518	3.854	4.266
	2. *Less:* Seed loss (10≥)	−0.375	−0.396	−0.410	−0.410	−0.452	−0.385	−0.427
	3. Net Production	3.379	3.567	3.694	3.686	4.066	3.469	3.839
	4. *Plus:* Imports	1.100	0.699	0.553	0.834	1.481	0.674	1.565
	5. *Less:* Exports	−0.006	−0.031	−0.007	−0.007	−0.031	−0.016	−0.029
	6. Net availability	4.473	4.235	4.210	4.513	5.516	4.127	5.375
	7. Population (mill.)	46.2	47.4	48.6	49.9	51.1	52.5	54.0
	8. Per capita availability (lbs)	216.8	200.1	194.0	202.6	241.8	176.1	223.0
B.	*Rice:*							
	1. Official Production (mill. tons)	1.014	1.109	1.078	1.173	1.329	1.296	1.343
	2. *Less:* Seed loss (5≥)	−0.051	−0.055	−0.053	−0.059	−0.066	−0.065	−0.067
	3. Net Production	0.963	1.054	1.025	1.114	1.263	1.231	1.276
	4. *Less:* Exports	−0.236	−0.157	−0.462	−0.338	−0.114	−0.435	−0.417
	5. Net Availability	0.727	0.897	0.563	0.776	1.149	0.796	0.859
	6. Population (mill.)	46.2	47.4	48.6	49.9	51.1	52.5	54.0
	7. Per capita availability (lbs)	35.2	42.4	25.9	34.8	50.4	34.0	35.6

Source: Gary Hufbauer, "Cereal Consumption, Production, and Prices in West Pakistan," *Pakistan Development Review*, vol. 8 (Summer 1968), pp. 289–306.

Table 11–9 *Projected Wheat and Rice Demand—West Pakistan, 1966/67–1969/70*

A.	*Wheat*	*Quantity (mill. tons)*	*Lbs/Capita*
	1966/67	5.375	223.0
	1967/68	5.923	239.0
	1968/69	6.154	241.4
	1969/70	6.388	243.7
B.	*Rice*		
	1966/67	0.859	35.6
	1967/68	0.893	36.0
	1968/69	0.973	38.1
	1969/70	1.036	39.9

Assumptions: Population growth rate = 2.8%. Income growth rate = See table 10. Price changes: (a) wheat: 1966/67–1967/68 = −10%; 1967/68—no change. (b) rice: 1966/67–1967/68 = +5%; 1967/68–1968/69 = −5%; 1968/69–1969/70—no change.

Table 11–10 *Actual and Projected Growth Rates for Regional Income West Pakistan*

		(Per cent per annum)
Second Plan	1960/61–1964/65[a]	6.4
	1965/66 (actual)	4.5
	1966/67 (actual)	6.3
	1967/68 (actual)	8.0
	1968/69 (estimated)	6.0
	1969/70[b] (estimated)	5.8
Third Plan	1965/66–1969/70[c]	6.1
Fourth Plan	1970/71–1974/75	
	Assumption I[d]	6.0
	II	6.5
	III	7.0

Sources: [a] Planning Commission, Government of Pakistan. Annual Plan, 1968–69, pp. 9–10.
[b] Projected rate of growth required to meet Third Plan target of regional growth for West Pakistan of 6.1 per cent per annum.
[c] Planning Commission, Government of Pakistan. *The Third Five-Year Plan*, 1965–70, pp. 28–29.
[d] Planning Commission, Government of Pakistan: *Working Paper on the Fourth Five-Year Plan.*

Table 11–11   *Average Retail Price of Coarse Rice in East Pakistan*
(*Rs./maund*)

1955/56	Rs. 19.39
1956/57	31.32
1957/58	25.82
1958/59	24.85
1959/60	26.25
1960/61	24.32
1961/62	25.38
1962/63	27.10
1963/64	23.84
1964/65	25.06
1965/66	29.66
1966/67	38.73
1967/68	34.66
1968/69	38.36

Source: Government of East Pakistan: Food Department.

Table 11–12   *Rice Production in East Pakistan (1000's of tons)*

1955/56	6,384
1956/57	8,185
1957/58	7,598
1958/59	6,921
1959/60	8,482
1960/61	9,519
1961/62	9,466
1962/63	8,730
1963/64	10,456
1964/65	10,337
1965/66	10,335
1966/67	9,424
1967/68	10,995
1968/69	10,900

Source: *20 Years of Pakistan in Statistics.*

Notes to Figure 11–1: 1. The horizontal axis on this diagram is time, that is, month of the year; the vertical axis is percentage of crop intensity. Choosing any one month and ranging vertically on the diagram, one can see the proportion of land used for each purpose. The lines between different crops are diagonal because it is impossible to shift all the land from one crop to another instantaneously.

2. Consider this diagram to be representative of a farm of ten *cultivated* acres. If there was sufficient irrigation water, it might be possible to double crop, that is, 10 acres would be planted in the Spring, and these same 10 acres replanted in the Fall, making a total of 20 *cropped* acres. Under the old system, there was insufficient water and land was not a binding constraint. In other words, there was some fallow throughout the year. Under the new system with supplemental water, land now becomes binding. There is fallow only in one season and only then if the length of the growing season for certain crops, such as cotton, is so long that a fall crop cannot be planted. The new cropping pattern is simply illustrative. Were the prices of say rice and wheat "very" high, there would be a tendency for these crops to drive out all others, and also for them to eliminate all the fall-season fallow.

Figure 11–1

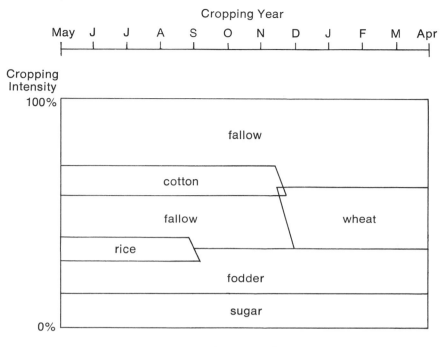

'Old' Cropping Pattern

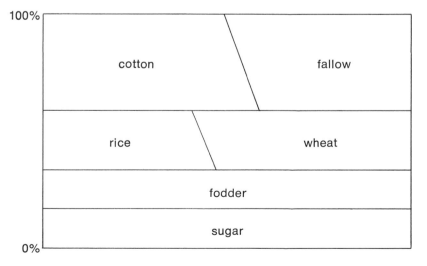

'New' Cropping Pattern

Suggested Readings

The student is expected to be familiar with starred (*) items.

1. Lewis, S. R., Jr. "Domestic Resources and Fiscal Policy in Pakistan's Second and Third Plans." *Pakistan Development Review,* vol. 5, Autumn 1965, pp. 461–485.

2. ———. "Effects of Trade Policy on Domestic Relative Prices: Pakistan, 1951–1964." *American Economic Review,* vol. 58, March 1968, pp. 60–78.

3. Rabbani, A. K. M. Ghulam. "Economic Determinants of Jute Production in India and Pakistan." *Pakistan Development Review,* vol. 5, Summer 1965, pp. 191–228.

4. *Papanek, Gustav F. *Pakistan's Development: Social Goals and Private Incentives.* Cambridge: Harvard University Press, 1967, chapter VI.

5. Falcon, Walter P., and Gotsch, Carl H. "Lessons in Agricultural Development—Pakistan." Edited by G. F. Papanek. *Development Policy: Theory and Practice.* Cambridge: Harvard University Press, 1968.

6. *———. "Relative Price Response, Economic Efficiency and Technological Change: A Case Study of Punjab Agriculture." Edited by W. P. Falcon and G. F. Papanek. *Development Policy II: The Pakistan Experience.* Cambridge: Harvard University Press, 1971.

7. Hufbauer, Gary C. "West Pakistan Exports: Effective Taxation, Policy Promotion, and Sectoral Descrimination." Edited by W. P. Falcon and G. F. Papanek. *Development Policy II: The Pakistan Experience.* Cambridge: Harvard University Press, 1971.

8. Lewis, S. R., Jr., and Guisinger, Stephen. "Measuring Protection in a Developing Country: The Case of Pakistan." *Journal of Political Economy.* August, 1968.

9. Pal, Mati Lal. "The Determinants of the Domestic Prices of Imports." *Pakistan Development Review,* vol. 4, Winter 1964, pp. 596–622.

10. ———. "Domestic Prices of Imports in Pakistan: Extension of Empirical Findings." *Pakistan Development Review,* vol. 5, Winter 1965, pp. 547–585.

11. Alamgir, M. "The Domestic Prices of Imported Commodities in Pakistan: A Further Study." *Pakistan Development Review,* vol. 7, Spring 1968, pp. 35–73.

12. *Gotsch, Carl H. "A Programming Approach to Some Agriculture Policy Problems in West Pakistan." *Paksitan Development Review,* vol. 8, Summer 1968, pp. 192–221.

Case 12: Consistency and Planning: The Use of Macromodels

Preparation of a medium term plan, usually covering a five-year period, is a process normally initiated two or three years before the plan period is to begin. Initial work on the plan requires some ideas, admittedly often very rough, on the economic and social goals of the nation. Usually such national objectives are embodied in the plethora of statements made by the national leaders. Insofar as these statements become accepted as the nation's goals, it remains for the planners to reconcile the desirable and the feasible and to eliminate conflicting objectives.

After some rough guidelines have been mapped out, the actual work on the plan documents involves an amount of detail that can quickly lead to a staggering amount of fruitless work. The experience of the Pakistan Planning Commission in its work on preparing the Third Five-Year Plan (TFYP) for 1965–1970 is instructive.

In 1962/63, when preliminary work on the TFYP began, the performance of the economy during the Second Plan period was only partially known and the economy appeared to be growing very slowly. In part this reflected the fact that given the gestation period for investment, the expected increases in output had not yet made themselves felt and also there was a considerable time lag in the collection and publication of statistics. Early statements on the TFYP called for a growth rate of 5.4 per cent per annum and general suggestions that the economy would have to make major strides in meeting a number of long-run national objectives: to reduce dependence on foreign aid so that all external assistance could be eliminated by 1985; to achieve self-sufficiency in food production; to reduce the regional inequalities in income, primarily those between East and West Pakistan so that equal per capita regional income levels would be achieved by 1985; and to raise per capita incomes by 2.7 per cent over the next five years.

Given these broad directives various sections of the Planning Commission set to work. The Fiscal and Monetary section prepared estimates of resource availabilities and, given some estimates of potential investment requirements, thus came up with an estimate of the domestic resources gap. At the same time, and working rather independently, the International Economics section projected probable exports for the period 1965–70, estimated import requirements, in a somewhat haphazard manner, and came up with a foreign exchange gap. Then, recognizing the requirement to move towards self-sufficiency, it was decided that this foreign exchange gap would have to be reduced by pushing for import substitution. Working in virtual isolation other sections dutifully began to stake out their claims to resources and to project the contribution these economic sectors would make to overall growth. Thus the Industries section, utilizing completed project reports, feasibility and engineering studies, began to prepare an industries investment program. Little attention was paid to the projected requirement for import substitution, the likely impact on import demand of alternative projects or the availability of required inputs from such national sectors as transportation and electricity. Similarly, the Agriculture section projected agricultural growth rates with scant awareness of the projected export requirements for cotton and jute. Other sections dealing with transportation, water and power, housing, and education all continued to fill in the necessary numbers and set forth the policy suggestions that eventually make up a plan.

The various papers prepared by the individual sections eventually found their way to the office of the Chief Economist and the Perspective Planning section. Even a cursory reading of these projections and proposals revealed their basic inconsistency. While a series of meetings between section chiefs did lead to some better understanding of what was feasible, and some elimination of inconsistencies, the revised sectoral programs still failed to add up to a consistent whole.

To compound confusion, it became apparent, late in 1963, that the economy was growing at an astonishing rate. The breakthrough in agricultural production, combined with a rapidly growing industrial sector, made it clear that much of the specific work on the TFYP was already dated. The growth rate for GNP so cautiously set at 5.9 per cent for 1970 would be reached, in all likelihood, by 1965. Similarly, exports would, by the end of the Second Plan period (1965), exceed the targets set for the next plan period; as would the rate of industrial and agricultural growth. With time running out, the TFYP was no nearer completion than it had been 18 months before.

It was at this juncture that the Perspective Planning section began construction of a medium term consistency model. Although at first the idea of "mechanically grinding out" a Third Plan led to some resistance within the Planning Commission to this project, the actual model, and its careful use, soon made zealots out of skeptics. The model (see (6) in the Suggested Readings) was based primarily on an interindustry table for 1959–60, updated by using the latest Census of Manufacturing Industries data, aggregated to seven sectors. (Since Pakistan then did not have a computer the model had to be solved by using less elegant computational tools. Hence the need to keep the sectoral detail to manageable proportions.) In addition, the model specified a number of policy variables and exogenous variables, so that alternative targets and policies could be quickly explored as to their impact on the economy as a whole (see (7) in the Suggested Readings). Although this model had a number of shortcomings, it proved useful in many ways. It permitted an identification of sensitive variables; could quickly interpret the impact of new targets which were set as actual data on the Second Five-Year Plan began to replace projections; ensured a minimal degree of sectoral consistency; and reconciled sectoral requirements with macroeconomic targets. And as an external benefit, one not to be dismissed too lightly, it gave a sound and economically respectable basis to the TFYP which eventually made that document more "salable" to the aid givers in what became increasingly a tight aid market.

By late 1967 preliminary work on the Fourth Five-Year Plan (1970–75) was begun by the Planning Commission. While the experience gained during the drafting of the TFYP left little doubt that some econometric model would be used again, the precise form of such model was still very much in doubt and under debate within the Commission. In addition the Commission was now better staffed and thus capable of applying increasingly complex techniques. (A computer was also available in Pakistan.) Finally a number of models dealing specifically with Pakistan had been built over the past few years and there was reason to believe that one of these models could, and should, be used, albeit after some revision, thus greatly easing the amount of work to be done in the time available. There was an aggregate linear programming model (see (2) in the Suggested Readings). Building on this work regional and sectoral detail had been added in another effort (see (5) in the Suggested Readings). A simulation model had been tested (see (4) in the Suggested Readings). This simulation model, an outgrowth of a much more ambitious model constructed for Colombia, was relatively simple, but had the advantage that it could be readily extended by drawing upon the full Colombia model. Work on an econometric model had already begun in Pakistan, but this in no way foreclosed the issue. Although the precise shape of the last model was still unknown, it appeared to be similar to a model constructed for Greece (see (1) in the Suggested Readings). And there are those who would continue to use the TFYP model, perhaps in a somewhat revised and updated version.

In reaching a decision on what type of model to use the Planning Commission should take into account a number of factors. Although data availability in Pakistan has improved since 1965, data are still a scarce commodity. (The most recent Census of Manufacturing is for 1963/64, but is only partially tabulated.) The model should permit easy identification of policy variables and be readily solvable for alternative values of such parameters. The rapid technological change characterizing the Pakistan economy should be reflected in the model. Any model used must become operative quickly if it is to make a major contribution to the preparation of the Fourth Five-Year Plan. Also the number of economists who can be spared to work on the model probably does not exceed two or three man-year equivalents. And, perhaps most important, the model results must be comprehensible to the policy makers.

What then are the pros and cons of each model? How far should the Commission opt for a model that ensures consistency but neglects optimality? Should the model reflect both long-run and short-run objectives? Or does the weakness of the underlying data, so often emphasized by all the authors of the various Pakistan models, mean that such exercises are basically futile in any case? If so, what alternatives does the Planning Commission have?

Suggested Readings

The student is expected to be familiar with starred (*) items.

1. Adelman, Irma, and Chenery, H. B. "Foreign Aid and Economic Development: The Case of Greece." *The Review of Economics and Statistics,* vol. 48, February 1966, pp. 1–19.

2. Chenery, Hollis B., and MacEwan, A. "Optimal Patterns of Growth and Aid: The Case of Pakistan." *Pakistan Development Review,* vol. 6, Summer 1966, pp. 209–242. Also reprinted in: I. Adelman and E. Thorbecke. *The Theory and Design of Economic Development.* Baltimore: Johns Hopkins Press, 1966, pp. 209–242. (A suggested alternative reading is: Chenery, Hollis B. and Strout, A. "Foreign Aid and Economic Development." *American Economic Review,* vol. 56, September 1966, pp. 679–733.

3. *Conrad, Alfred H. "Econometric Models in Development Planning—Pakistan, Argentina, Liberia." *Development Policy: Theory and Practice.* Edited by G. F. Papanek. Cambridge: Harvard University Press, 1968, pp. 31–54.

4. Kresge, David. "A Simulation Model for Economic Planning: A Pakistan Example." Economic Development Reports, no. 81. Cambridge: Development Advisory Service, 1967. Mimeographed.

5. *Stern, Joseph J. "Growth, Development and Regional Equity in Pakistan." *Development Policy II: The Pakistan Experience.* Edited by Walter P. Falcon and Gustav F. Papanek. Harvard University Press, 1971.

6. Tims, Wouter. *Analytical Techniques for Development Planning: A Case Study of Pakistan's Third Five-Year Plan (1965–1970).* Karachi, Pakistan: Pakistan Institute of Development Economics, 1968.

7. *———. "A Growth Model and Its Application." *Development Policy: Theory and Practice.* Edited by G. F. Papanek. Cambridge: Harvard University Press, 1968, pp. 3–30.

8. Jarrett, Frank G. "Models for Pakistan's Fourth Plan." Economic Development Reports, no. 110. Cambridge: Development Advisory Service, 1968. Mimeographed.

9. Stern, Joseph J. "An Evaluation of Inter-Industry Research on Pakistan." Economic Development Reports, no 120. Cambridge: Development Advisory Service, 1968. Mimeographed.

10. *Vernon, Raymond. "Comprehensive Model-Building in the Planning Process: The Case of the Less-Developed Economies." *Economic Journal,* vol. 76, March 1966, pp. 57–69.

11. Hirschman, Albert O. *Development Projects Observed.* Washington: The Brookings Institution, 1967, chapter 1.

12. Papanek, Gustav F. "Development Theory and DAS Experience," *Development Policy: Theory and Practice.* Edited by G. F. Papanek. Harvard University Press, 1968.

Case 13: Development Strategies and the Role of Government

In addition to deciding on the overall magnitude of the Fourth Five-Year Plan (1970–1975) the Pakistan Planning Commission must also deal with several broad strategy questions. The macromodel which is expected to provide some guidance on the general magnitudes may also be helpful on some strategy questions. For some of these issues, however, the model is too simple to provide any guidance and on all of them it is inadequate to make conclusive decisions.

The first major question of strategy is the relative allocation of scarce resources to broad purposes and sectors. All the sections of the Planning Commission, dealing with various sectors of the economy, and all Ministries and Departments insist on having some indication of the broad magnitudes with respect to the size of their budgets before they begin their detailed work on project and program preparations. Before the Planning Commission can give some indication whether education, for instance, will get 5 per cent or 20 per cent of the total financial resources, it must be reasonably clear in its own mind what development strategy it wishes to pursue.

The second broad issue to be considered is the perennial question of the extent and nature of government intervention in the economy. While others may be concerned with ideological arguments, the Planning Commission is determined to limit itself to a consideration of the economic facets of the issue.

Development Strategy

With respect to strategy the *first question,* admittedly asked only by a few people who have been exposed to some of the literature in the development field, is whether the current strategy is, and the future strategy should be, one of "balanced" or "unbalanced" growth. One could argue that the current strategy, which assumes that exports and industrial output will grow more rapidly than the Domestic Product, is an unbalanced growth strategy. On the other hand one could argue that the distribution of investment resources over a variety of fields plus the diversification of exports suggest a balanced growth strategy.

Some analysts suggest that the essence of a balanced growth strategy is a maximum reliance on domestic production to meet domestic demand. Unbalanced growth, in their view, implies a greater confidence in the benefits of comparative advantage and international trade; in other words, a strategy which emphasizes exports of those goods which a country is best equipped to produce cheaply and reliance on imports to meet much of the internal demand. The issue, as these analysts see it, is very much that originally posed by Nurske—autarchy and import substitution versus international trade and export specialization. Autarchy avoids the risks of international trade, especially the risk that developed countries will find substitutes for or restrict the import of goods which the less developed countries produce. Export specialization, on the other hand, permits a country to benefit from comparative advantage and economies of scale.

Another, small, group of analysts see the issue in terms of the analysis posited by Hirschman. On the one hand balanced growth has the advantage of avoiding waste due to bottlenecks, while unbalanced growth is desirable because it forces decisions to break bottlenecks. Unbalanced growth inceases decision making ability, the scarcest resource in a less developed country, according to its advocates.

First, it is necessary to define the meaning of the terms "balanced" and "unbalanced" growth; second, to indicate which strategy Pakistan is following; and third, to decide which strategy it should follow. The definitional issue is not a crucial one, but as economists have devoted considerable thought and ingenuity to a debate on the advantage of "balanced" versus "unbalanced" growth, some people in Pakistan are curious about the appropriate classification for their country. The question of the appropriate strategy to follow is important in its own right.

The *second question* with respect to strategy is the issue of relative emphasis on rural and urban investment. Again there has been much argument on the relative priority to be given to increasing agricultural output (by expenditure on agriculture, irrigation and rural roads, by subsidies on agricultural inputs, and by higher prices for agricultural products) as against industrial output (by investment in industry, urban infrastructure, power for industry, technical education, and by higher prices for industrial products). This issue has not only agitated the development profession, but also decision makers in Pakistan. On the one hand, those who argue for more investment in agriculture point out that:

1. The capital/output ratio in agriculture is much more favorable than in industry.

2. The bulk of foreign exchange is earned and will in the future have to be earned by agricultural products, including those lightly processed.

3. Given the preponderance of agriculture in the Domestic Product, no conceivable growth in industry can make for an acceptable rate of per capita growth, unless agriculture is given sufficient priority to grow substantially more rapidly than population.

On the other hand, the advocates of industry, and especially of the capital goods industry, argue that:

1. Development means industrialization; the essence of the development process is the transfer of labor from agriculture, with a low labor productivity, to industry, with a high labor productivity. The more rapid is industrial growth, the more rapid will be development.

2. Agricultural exports face a declining and fluctuating market; industry will provide the goods that now have to be imported. Pakistan especially needs to develop the capital or producer goods industries so that an

increasing share of the rapidly growing demand for such goods can be met from domestic supplies.

3. Increased agricultural output goes primarily to improve consumption levels; a high proportion of increased industrial output is saved, particularly if profits are high (the Galenson-Leibenstein arguments).

Only industrial development can therefore provide the resources to step up the rate of savings/investment and therefore of growth.

Arguments on both sides seem plausible. The question whether the Plan should provide resources for agriculture at the expense of industry, or vice versa, is too important, however, to be settled on the basis of plausibility. The terms of trade have been very favorable for agriculture in the last few years, but with the good harvest of 1967/68 they threaten to turn sharply against it.

Three questions arise in connection with the Fourth Plan: (a) what professional criteria, if any, are available to decide on the relative priority of agriculture and industry; (b) should the Fourth Plan have a larger, smaller or unchanged relative allocation for agriculture and industry than the Third (on the assumption that the Fourth Plan will be one-third larger than the Third in terms of total investment); (c) should the government intervene to improve the terms of trade for agriculture (industry); if so, how and to what extent.[1]

The *third question,* equally important, is the relative allocation for "investment in human capital." (A particularly obnoxious and misleading aspect of the new terminology of economic development, almost as bad as "developing countries." It implies on the one hand that expenditure on human beings has to be justified in the same way as expenditure on machines, and on the other that all such expenditures are productive in economic terms). One group argues that past Plans neglected expenditure on human beings, especially education. Their arguments included the following points:

1. An educated population will know how to acquire and use machines, while machines do not as yet know how to acquire an educated population. The correlation between educational attainment and income levels is positive and very high throughout the world. Japan and the USSR are particularly clear examples of rapid economic growth and high priority to education. Lack of education may be the most serious constraint on future growth.

2. Literacy and reasonable health are required to spread improved technology, especially in the rural areas.

3. The popular demand is for more education and better health. For the sake of political support, important for development as well as the government's survival, these demands have to be met.

[1] The information made available, and the analysis developed for Case 11 is obviously relevant here.

The opponents of a higher allocation for education and health also have cogent arguments. They note that:

1. These "social service" expenditures (opponents do not call them "investment") are not directly productive. Pakistan can not afford to spend more money on them. It might end up with an educational and health establishment that required greatly increased resources to maintain and stagnant "directly productive" sectors unable to support these social services.

2. Changes in technology depend more on economic incentives, institutions for disseminating information and the availability of capital, than on general education or better health. "The factory is the most effective school" they argue.

3. In political terms, more education might be demanded, but in fact it only contributes to political instability. Marxists are correct when they call the unemployed intellectuals (or semi-intellectuals) the "officers of the revolution."

On this problem, too, there seem to be plausible arguments on both sides. The question remains whether in comparison with the Third Plan, a shift of resources to or from the social sectors can be justified in the Fourth Plan.

The *fourth question* of strategy has raised more political dust than the other three combined—the relative allocation of resources to East and West Pakistan. One of the development objectives, of sufficient importance to be covered in the Constitution, is to achieve regional parity in per capita income. This requires a more rapid rate of growth in East Pakistan, and the Third Plan proposed to achieve a slightly higher rate of growth in that Province. The question then is the extent to which the Fourth Plan should further shift the allocation of resources in favor of East Pakistan.

It is argued that the allocation of resources to East Pakistan is already so much larger than past programs in that Province that administrative and institutional arrangements will be inadequate to use effectively even the resources planned during the Third Plan period. Yet these resources were made available only by reducing the commitment of public resources for West Pakistan to a level below the capacity of its administrative and institutional framework. It would then be in the interest of Pakistan's overall development to reduce the allocation of government resources to East Pakistan, which could use them only inefficiently, in order to increase them for West Pakistan, which badly needs them. The objective of parity need not be forgotten, just deferred a bit longer. The costs of achieving such per capita income parity by 1985 have been measured by Stern (see (11) in the Suggested Readings) and found to be very significant. This study concluded that the country as a whole could be made better off if these costs were avoided by postponing or modifying the regional parity goal.

On the other hand, it is argued that the allocation to East Pakistan is inadequate. It is clear from the capital/output ratios as shown in the Third Plan, that investment in East Pakistan yields a higher return than in West Pakistan. Therefore all the talk of limited administrative and institutional capacity in East Pakistan is so much nonsense—the rate of return on investment in East Pakistan is not lower but actually higher than in West Pakistan. Furthermore, despite the fact that per capita income is lower in East Pakistan, what little information is available suggests that its rate of savings has been higher, at least in the 1960s, than in West Pakistan. This means that investment in East Pakistan will contribute more to growth than in West Pakistan, where a larger proportion of the increased output resulting from investment would be consumed (see (10) in the Suggested Readings). Hence it would be in the interest of Pakistan as a whole to increase the investment in East Pakistan further. This would give a higher rate of return, satisfy the objective of parity and have the further advantage of generating more savings.

The allocation of resources to the two provinces has important political overtones. The question remains whether economists have something to contribute to the discussion. What can one say about the economic costs and benefits of policies to shift a higher proportion of investment than in the past to East Pakistan? What policies and programs would be best suited to achieve such a shift?

Government Intervention

Pakistan has prided itself on a pragmatic mix of private enterprise and government intervention. The role of government during the Fourth Plan is to be decided on pragmatic grounds—what mix will best advance the major objectives of growth, equity and provincial parity.

Those favoring private enterprise argue that government is still too much involved in the economy. They point to the following:

1. The operation of plants by the two PIDC's (Pakistan Industrial Development Corporation) and other government agencies has been inefficient.

2. Government distribution of fertilizer, seeds, plant protection and credit has led to corruption and waste and has not been timely.

3. Import and investment controls distort the structure of production, introduce inefficiencies, lead to waste and corruption and do not provide the goods and services which are demanded by consumers.

4. High taxes on profits and income reduce incentives. Profits are also reduced by government controls which produce inefficiencies. As a result of lower profits and reduced incentives, savings are reduced. So is foreign private investment.

They have evidence for all the points they make. They therefore suggest a free enterprise economy as the goal for the Fourth Five-Year Plan. Government intervention should be limited to the usual areas of enforcing contracts, preventing or controlling monopolies, and ensuring justice. The aim is to achieve a pattern similar to countries such as Germany, the United States, and Japan, which have been very successful in terms of economic management. Savings would increase from their present low level as government interference with business and industry is reduced. Efficiency would improve since firms would be exposed to the full, icy, blast of competition. With savings and efficiency raised, growth would increase and eventually all segments of the society would be better off.

The opposition dismisses the free enterprise arguments as completely unrealistic and motivated by self-interest. They argue that a private enterprise economy never made much sense for Pakistan, but makes even less sense now that:

1. expected aid inflows are stagnant and are likely to decline,

2. the cheap, and easy gains in industrial development and exports have been achieved, and

3. the possibility for increased exports to the developed countries are becoming exhausted.

In addition, they point out that Pakistan has an insufficient number of entrepreneurs to run a free enterprise economy. Its introduction would, therefore, merely result in ever higher profits and capital export while the income distribution would steadily deteriorate.

Therefore, the government must now itself develop the heavy and import substituting industries required. Increased direct taxes are needed to squeeze savings out of agriculturalists, who are used to high incomes and consumption, and out of industrialists, who have experienced the joys of conspicuous consumption. Increased government ownership of industry is the only way to channel directly to the government the resources required for development and social justice. More direct controls over imports and investment are needed to avoid the waste of scarce resources on low priority, ill-considered, projects or for luxury purposes. In short, with resources scarce in relation to needs and with a high priority for social justice, direct intervention by the government needs to be increased, not decreased. The approach of Algeria, the U.A.R. and Cuba, is considered more appropriate for Pakistan than that followed by the developed countries.

The arguments are strongly held on both sides. What degree and kind of government intervention—both ownership and controls—should the Planning Commission recommend? Should the government reduce the areas of economic activity for which license and permits are required as well as its own investment activities? Or should these be increased? If it reduces these forms of direct intervention what, if anything, should be substituted?

Suggested Readings

In addition to the references on Pakistan provided in the first section and Cases 2 and 3, the following readings are relevant. The student is expected to be familiar with starred (*) items.

1. *Bell, David E. "Allocating Development Resources: Some Observations Based on the Pakistan Experience." *Public Policy,* vol. 9. Cambridge: Graduate School of Public Administration, Harvard University, 1959.

2. Cameron, Rondo. "Some Lessons of History for Developing Nations." *American Economic Review,* vol. 57, May 1967, pp. 312–324.

3. Higgins, Benjamin. "Development of the Labor Surplus Economy: Theory and Policy by John Fei and Gustav Ranis." *Economic Development and Cultural Change,* vol. 14, January 1966, pp. 237–247.

4. Hirschman, Albert O. *The Strategy of Economic Development.* New Haven: Yale University Press, 1958, chapters III and IV.

5. *Johnston, Bruce F., and Mellor, John W. "The Role of Agriculture in Economic Development." *American Economic Review,* vol. 51, September 1961, pp. 566–93.

6. *Lewis, W. Arthur. "On Assessing a Development Plan." *The Economic Bulletin* (of the Economic Society of Ghana), vol. 3, June–July 1959.

7. *Lipton, Michael. "Balanced and Unbalanced Growth in Underdeveloped Countries." *Economic Journal,* vol. 72, September 1962, pp. 641–57.

8. Nurkse, Ragnar. *Problems of Capital Formation in Underdeveloped Countries.* New York: Oxford University Press, 1962 (especially chapter I).

9. *Papanek, Gustav F. *Pakistan's Development: Social Goals and Private Incentives.* Cambridge: Harvard University Press, 1967 (especially chapter VIII).

10. *Rahman, Md. Anisur. *East and West Pakistan: A Problem in the Political Economy of Regional Planning.* Cambridge: Center for International Affairs, Occasional Paper No. 20, Harvard University, 1968.

11. Stern, Joseph J. "Growth, Development, and Regional Equity." Edited by Walter P. Falcon and Gustav F. Papanek. *Development Policy II: The Pakistan Experience.* Cambridge: Harvard University Press, 1971.